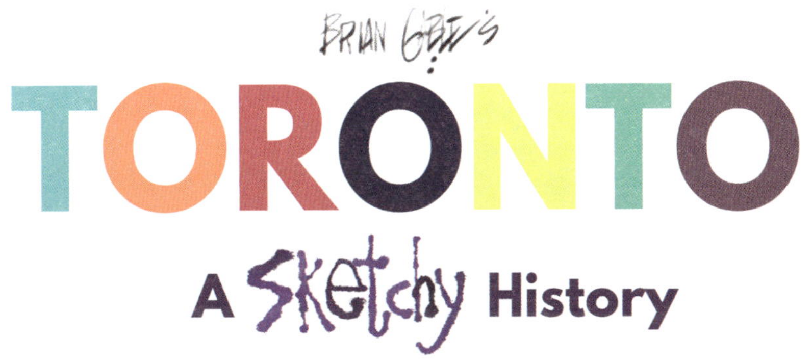
BRIAN GABLE'S
TORONTO
A Sketchy History

Sutherland House
416 Moore Ave., Suite 304
Toronto, ON M4G 1C9

First edition, February 2025

If you are interested in inviting one of our authors to a live event or media appearance, please contact sranasinghe@sutherlandhousebooks.com and visit our website at sutherlandhousebooks.com for more information.

We acknowledge the support of the Government of Canada.

Manufactured in China
Artwork designed by Brian Gable
Book composed by Karl Hunt

Library and Archives Canada Cataloguing in Publication
Title: Brian Gable's Toronto : a sketchy history.
Other titles: Toronto : a sketchy history
Names: Gable, Brian, 1949- author, artist
Identifiers: Canadiana (print) 20240519590 | Canadiana (ebook) 20240519620 |
ISBN 9781998365326 (softcover) | ISBN 9781998365333 (EPUB)
Subjects: LCSH: Toronto (Ont.)—History. | LCSH: Toronto (Ont.)—History—Pictorial works. |
LCGFT: Illustrated works.
Classification: LCC FC3097.4 .G33 2025 | DDC 971.3/54100222—dc23

ISBN 978-1-998365-32-6
eBook 978-1-998365-33-3

BRIAN GABLE'S

TORONTO

A Sketchy History

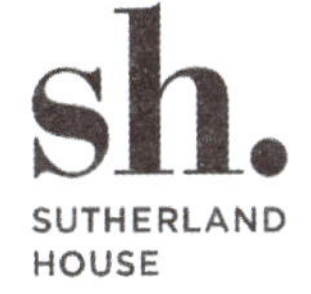

SUTHERLAND HOUSE

TORONTO, 2025

FOR BOWEN

"OUT OF THE CROOKED TIMBER OF HUMANITY,
NO STRAIGHT THING WAS EVER MADE."

IMMANUEL KANT

I first encountered the city of Toronto when I arrived there as a university student in 1970. Coming from Saskatoon, at that time a city of roughly 125,000, the immensity of Toronto was impressive. The opportunities to attend galleries, concerts, the variety of neighbourhoods and architecture were on a significantly larger scale than I was accustomed to. What came as a surprise was how blasé most Torontonians then seemed to feel about their metropolis. My enthusiasm stood in stark contrast to their indifference to and outright dismissal of the city's charms.

Over the next half century much of that indifference has faded and many citizens are now more likely to share some positive feelings about the place or at least acknowledge that the city has changed for the better in many ways.

Over the ensuing decades, I was fortunate to be able to visit a number of cities around the world. I quickly became fascinated by how unique each urban environment was. Like human beings, cities can be profoundly different in a wide range of aspects. How do these clusters of habitation develop such independent and immediately recognizable personalities?

The Welsh travel writer, Jan Morris, was also fascinated by this question. I first stumbled on to her work when I read essays that she wrote about both Saskatoon and Toronto. Her observations on both cities were a revelation to me and felt insightful and accurate. I read more. Her book, *Venice*, is regarded by many critics to be one of the finest portraits of that mysterious city. Her methodology has consistently been to avoid census tables and industrial statistics and replace these with on-the-ground personal observations. How do the citizens regard each other on the street? Do they wait for traffic lights? Does the city have a sense of excitement or is it generally forlorn?

Being a cartoonist, I instinctively knew that if I were to share thoughts about my home city I would best do it through drawing. My historian friends would no doubt be appalled that I didn't spend hours in archival research. Following Morris' example, I strove to communicate what it may have felt like and now feels like to live in this complicated and ever-changing metropolis.

With this in mind, I would like to salute the legacy of Jan Morris' many books which have opened our eyes to the wonder and variety of so many of this planet's complex and fascinating cities.

JAN MORRIS 1926-2020

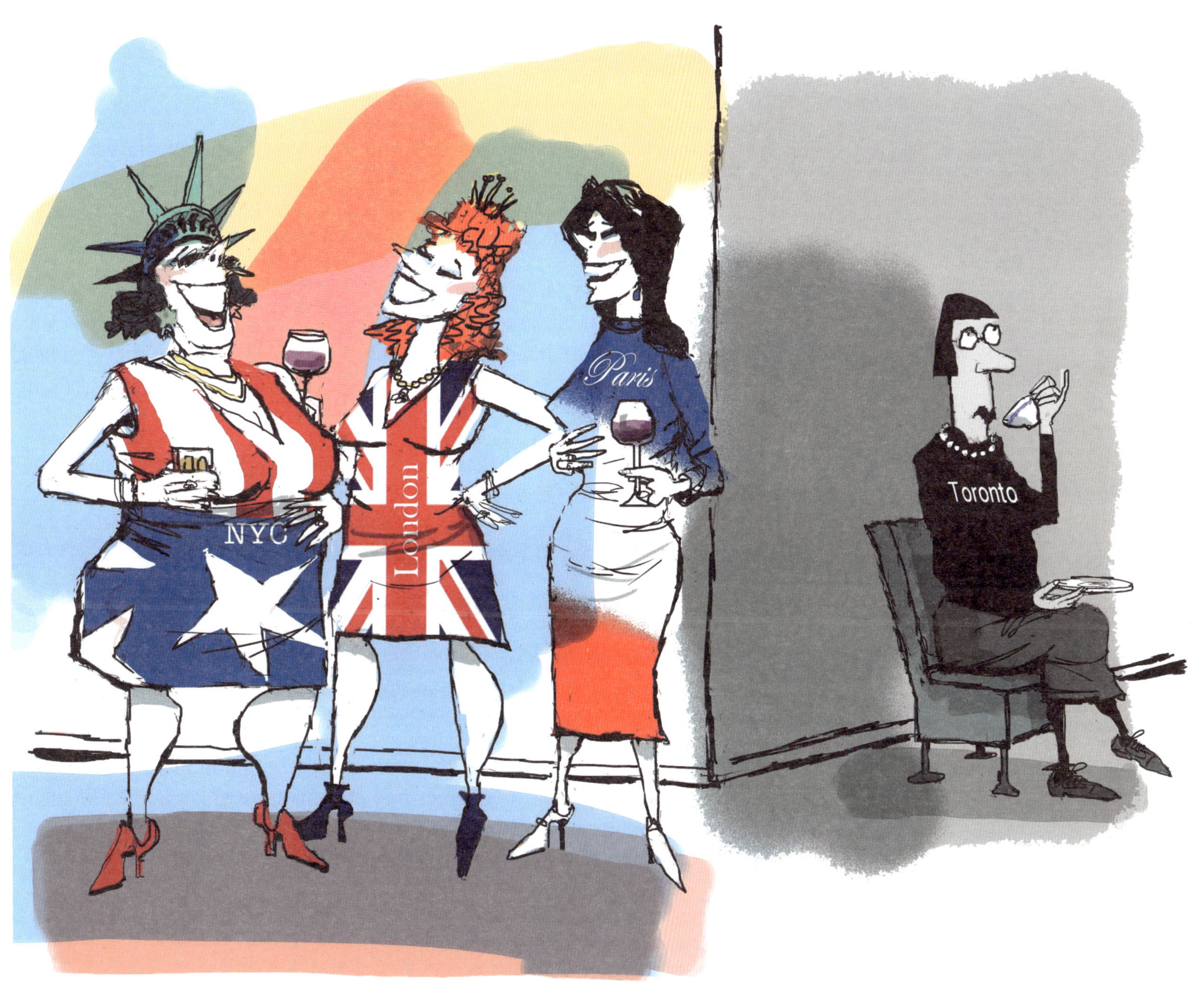
NYC
London
Paris
Toronto

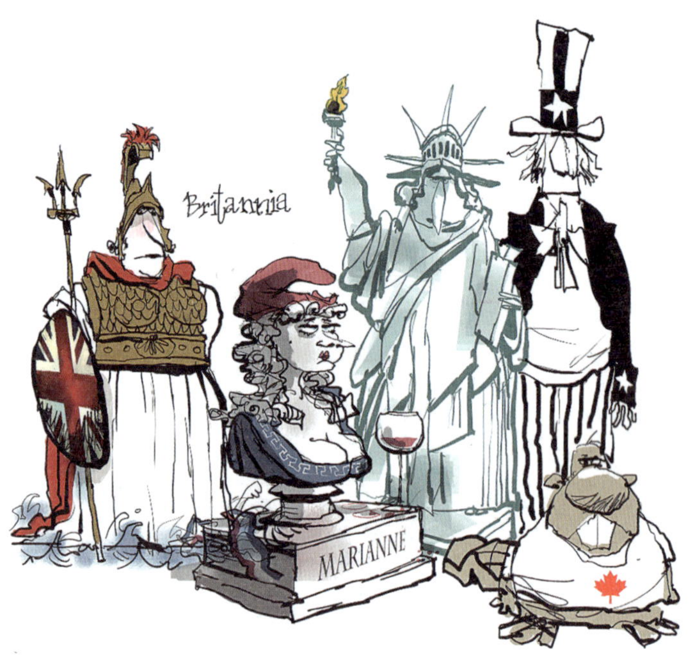

During my many years working as a newspaper editorial cartoonist I often drew figures who were symbols of their nation. Miss Liberty and Uncle Sam, Britannia, Marianne and of course, the stolid Canadian Beaver.

One day, after finishing a drawing and sending it off to press, I whimsically asked myself "What would a person symbolizing Toronto look like?" It seemed like an innocent enough question, and yet when I started the inevitable doodling process to find the right image, I came up blank.

There was no "there there", as Gertrude Stein said of her native Oakland, California.

So, what was essential soul of my city?

Other cities seemed easier to visualize. Paris; embodying elegance and romance. San Francisco; allegedly captivating visitors' hearts, Chicago; the city of broad shoulders, New York; sparking with hustle and attitude, London; an imperium encased in regal tradition and ceremony.

I even tried creating characters to represent Montreal and Vancouver. At least both these cities had personalities which many Canadians could agree on.

European attitude. Self-aware. Used to smoke Gitanes cigarettes. Loves to host festivals and is convinced only she knows how to make the very best bagels.

"Go Habs!"

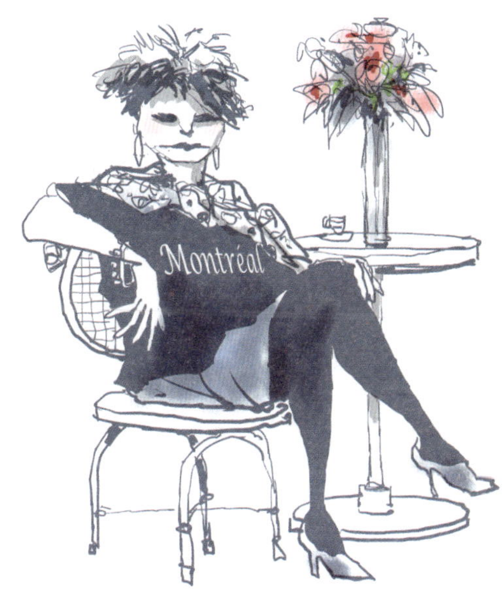

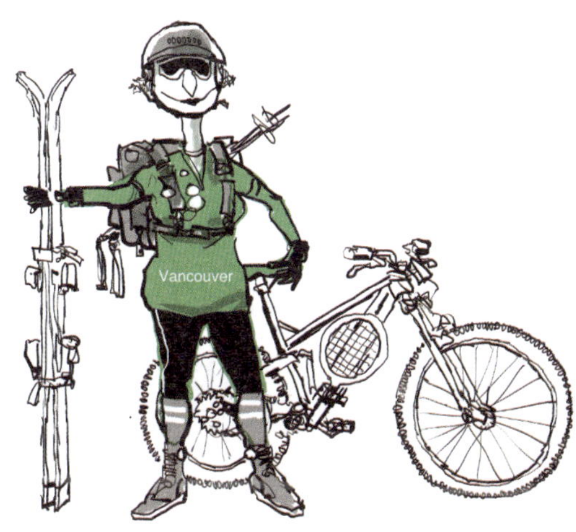

Owns an organic bamboo yoga mat. Adores bonding with her natural surroundings at every opportunity.

Meditates during breaks on mountain bike trails.

"Talk later...off to pilates".

Though she's changed dramatically over the years,
Toronto has always seemed to be, in essence, rather prim.

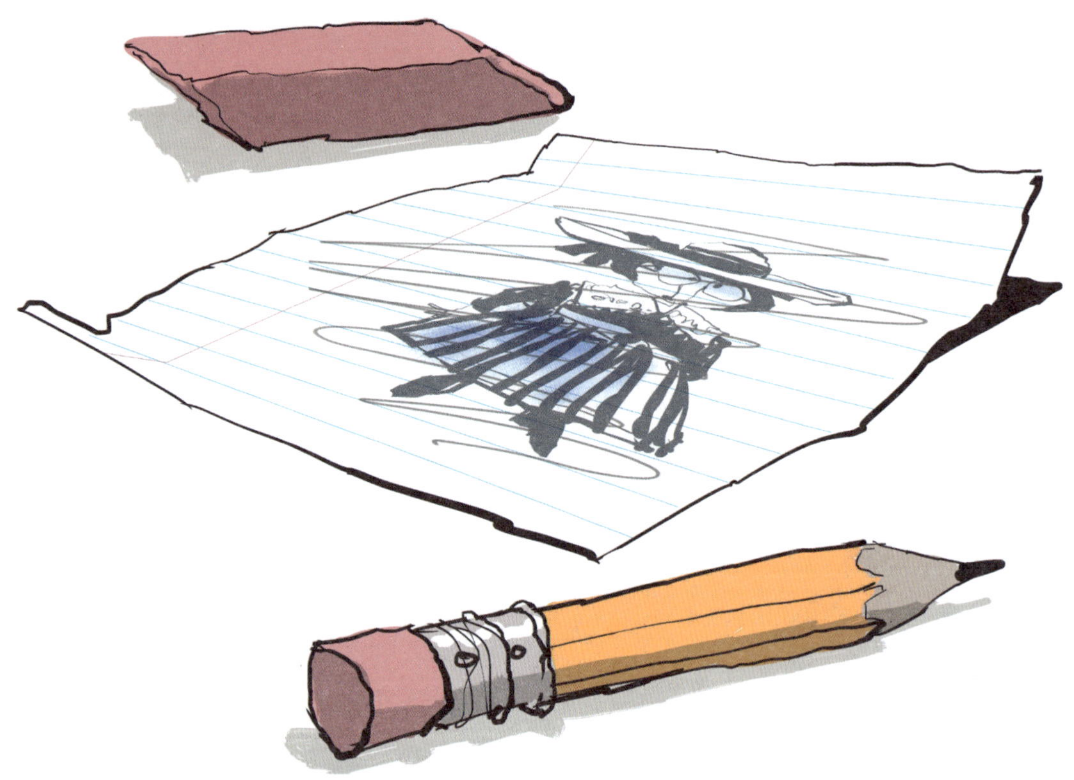

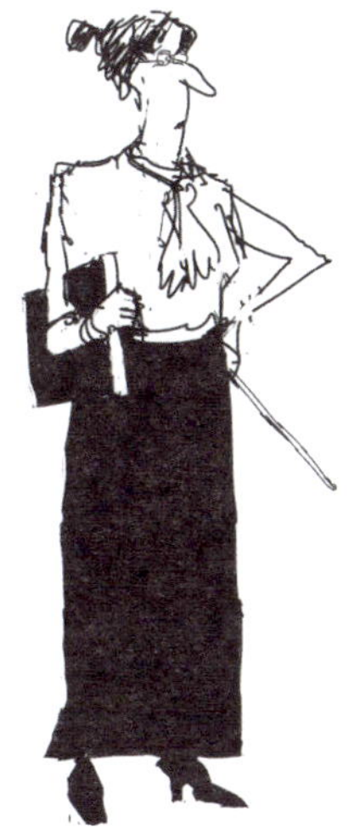

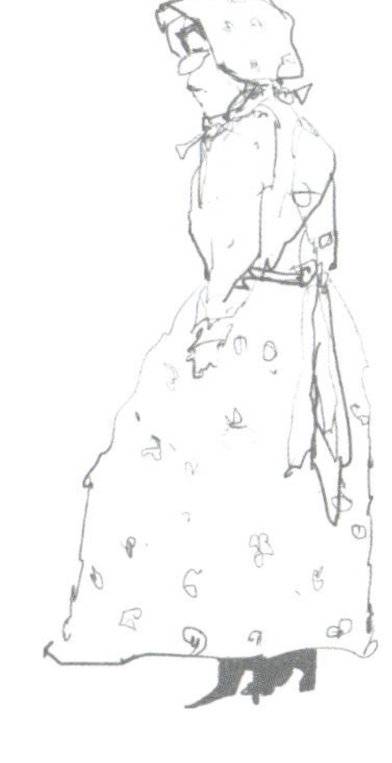

For much of her history, she exhibited a sense of Victorian propriety and restraint.

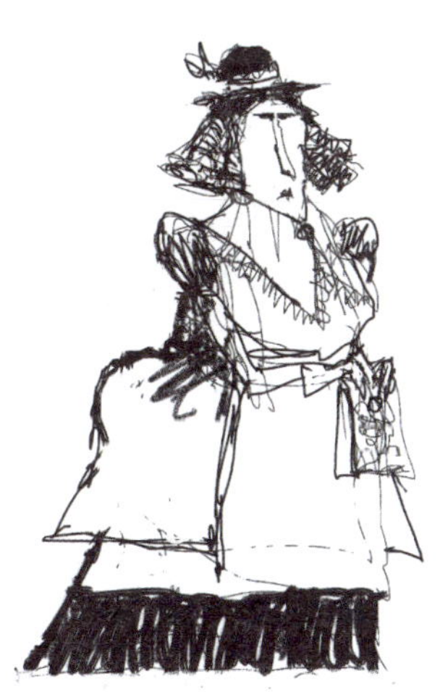

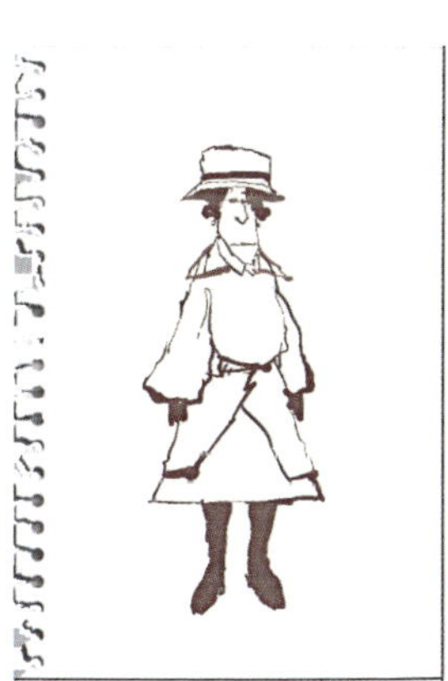

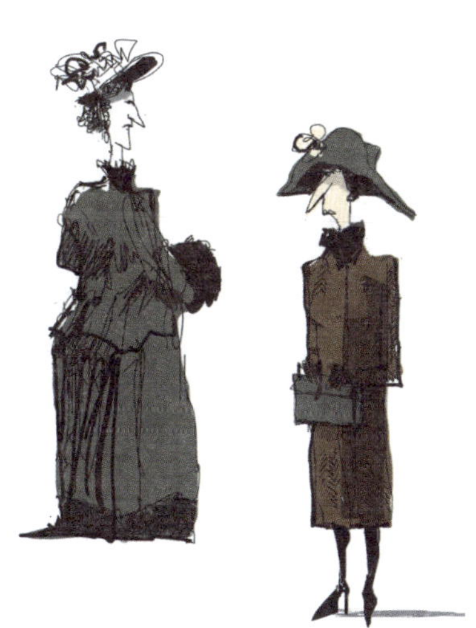

After hours of scribbling I was still coming up empty. Then, *voila!*

Toronto is a rather generic looking city. Other than the CN Tower and City Hall, there are few architectural monuments which impact on the global imagination.

So, the Toronto icon must embody the plain, the simple, the unadorned. She would be rather generic herself. Conservative clothing style, probably flannel and wool. Sensible shoes.

A woman devoted to a work ethic.

Underneath a dour surface, though, there is a certain resilience and the capacity to evolve over time. As well, she possesses a personality not entirely averse to new experiences.

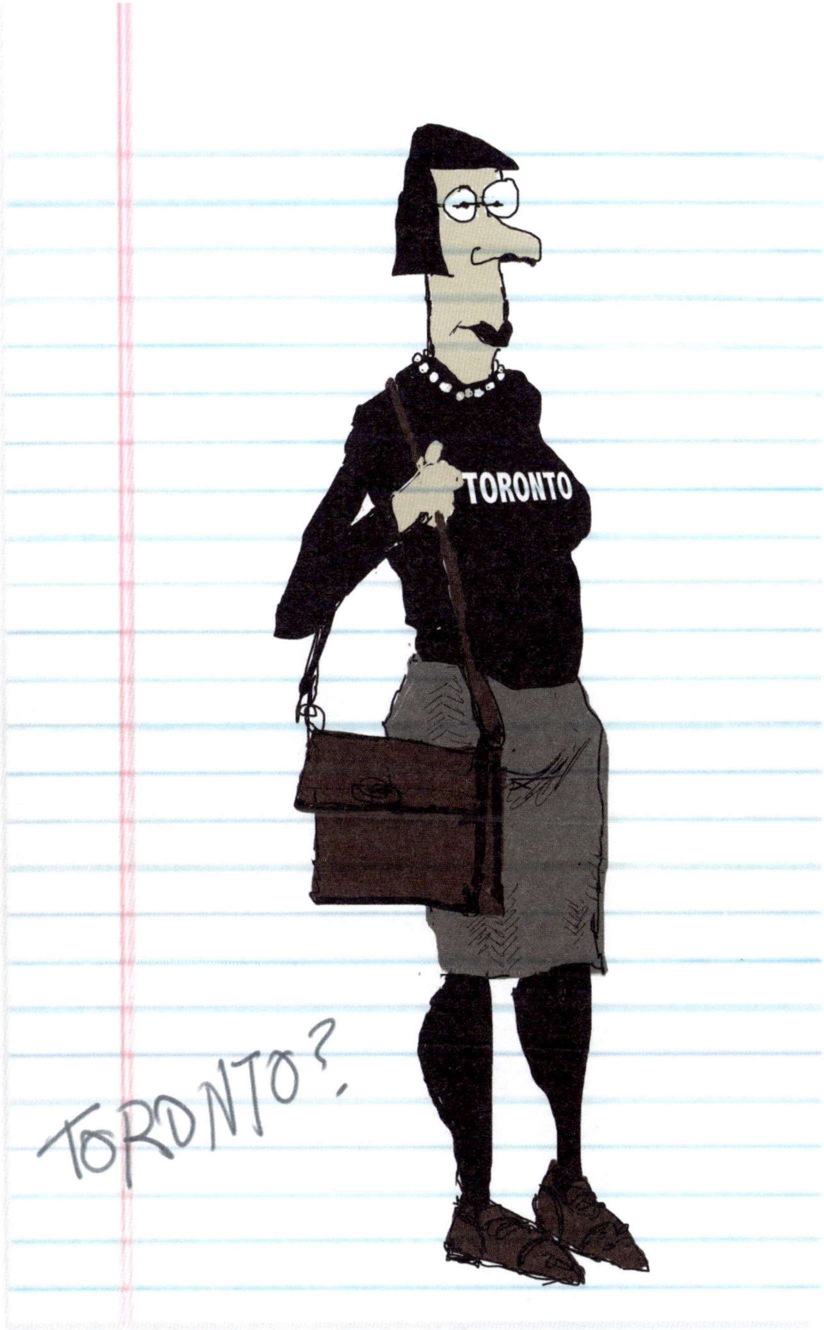

"YOUR HEART MAY NOT BE SINGING, AS YOU CONTEMPLATE THE PRESENCE AROUND YOU OF TORONTO THE GOOD, BUT IT SHOULD NOT BE SINKING EITHER. CHEER UP! YOU HAVE DRAWN SECOND PRIZE, I WOULD SAY, IN THE LOTTARIO OF LIFE."

JAN MORRIS

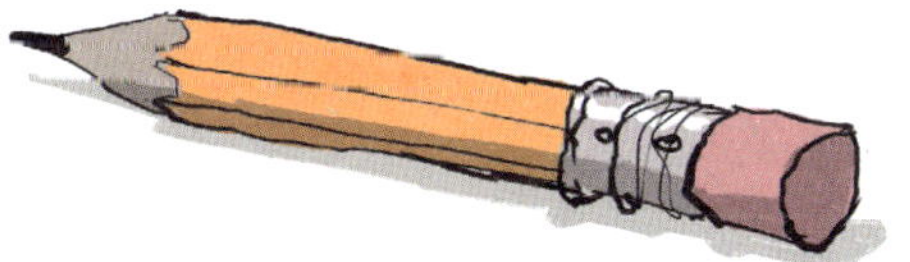

TORONTO: THE EARLY YEARS

In the beginning

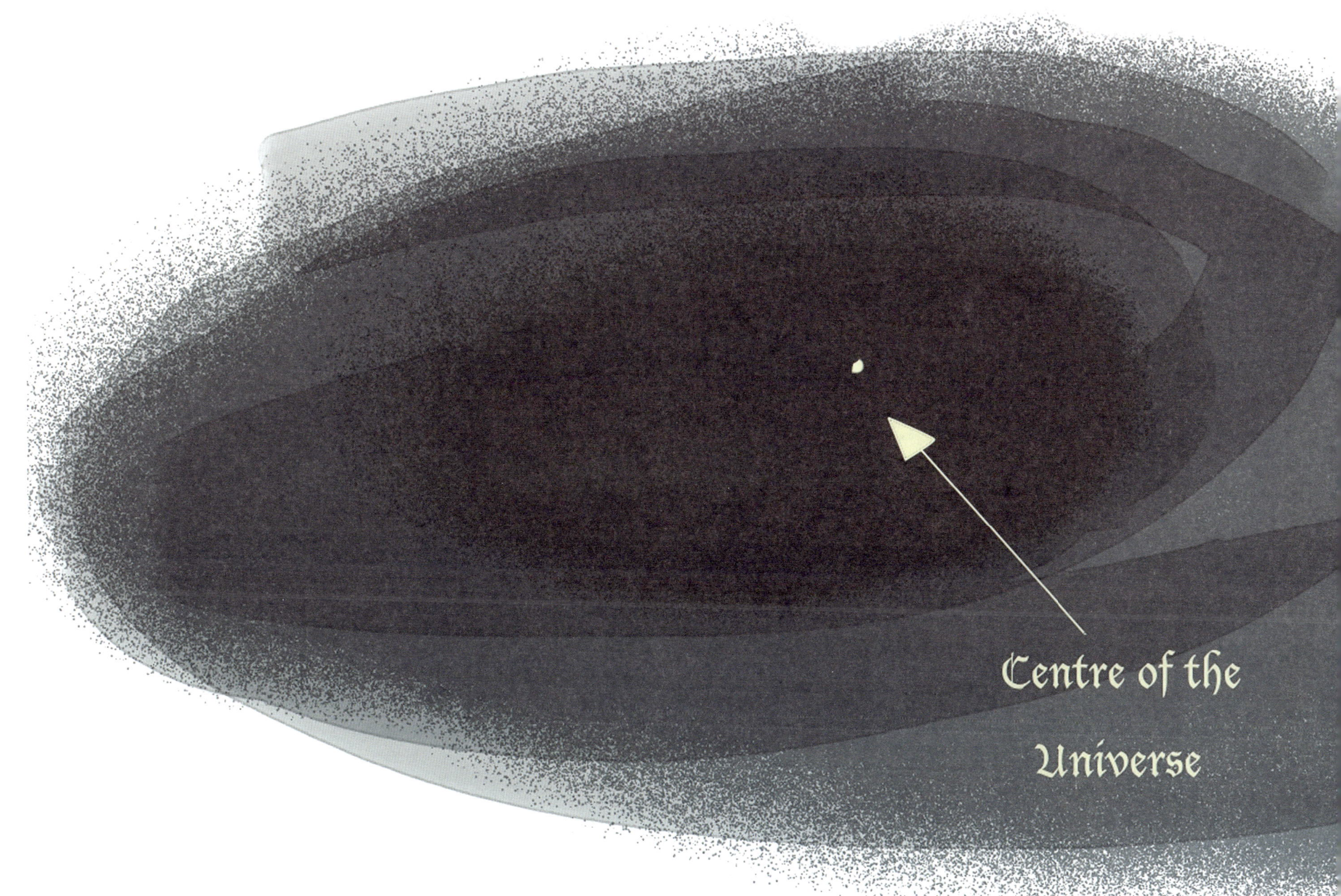
Centre of the
Universe

65 MILLION YEARS AGO: THE MESOZOIC ERA

The region now occupied by the city of Toronto has a tropical climate and is near earth's equator. Continental drift changes all that.

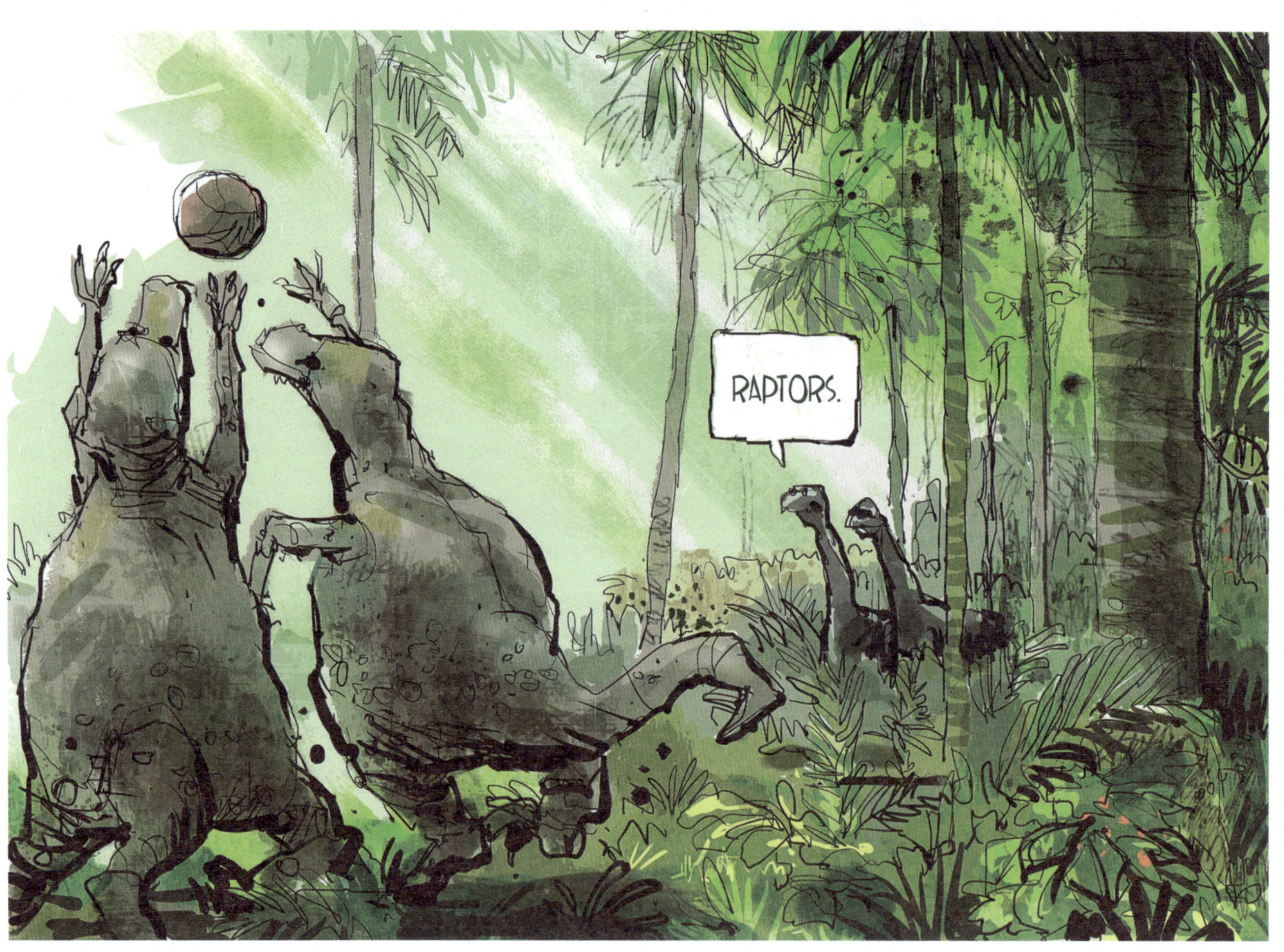

135,000 YEARS AGO: THE PLEISTOCENE ERA

Toronto lies under a gigantic glacier. There is no conclusive evidence that hockey is invented during this period.

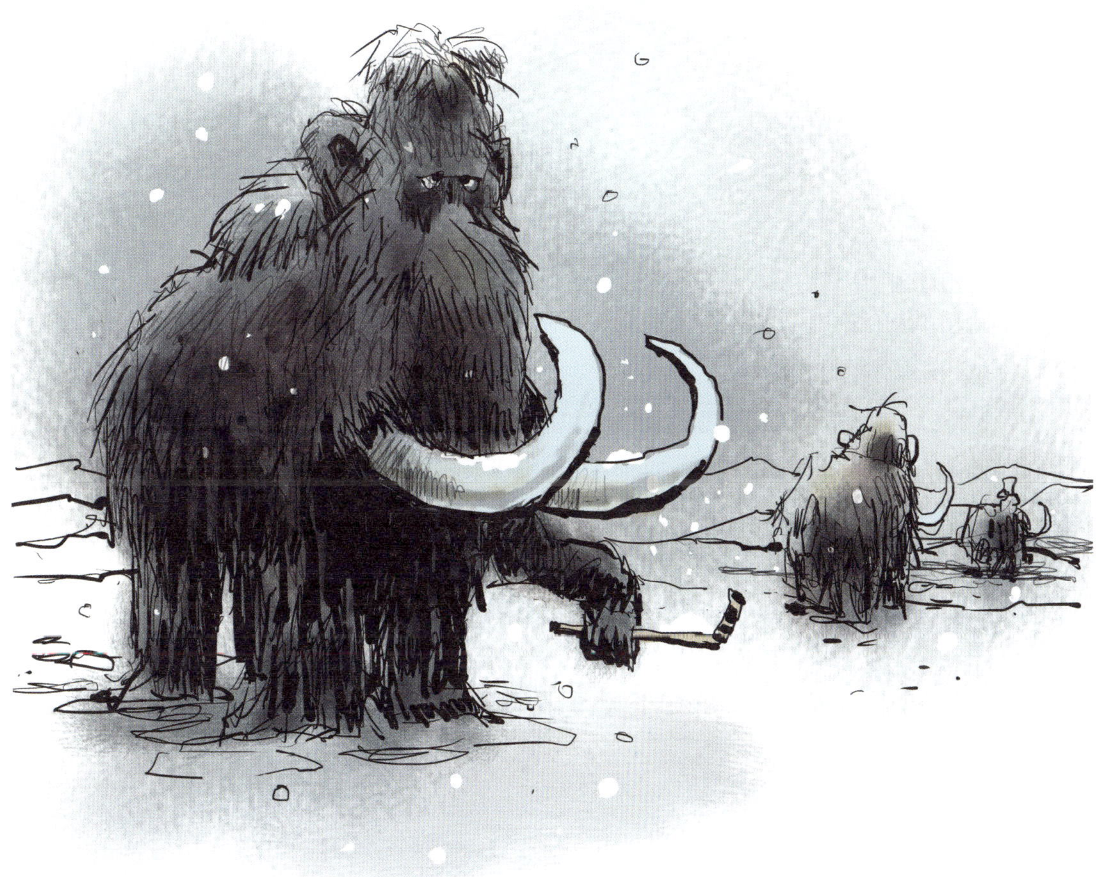

TORONTO CARRYING-PLACE TRAIL

For centuries, the abundant forests and rivers of the area now occupied by Toronto provide plentiful game and transportation routes for the First Nations who inhabit the region between Lake Huron and Lake Ontario.

A twenty-six mile trail from the mouth of the Humber River on Lake Ontario leads north to the Holland River near Lake Simcoe and ultimately to the Upper Great Lakes. This route becomes known as 'The Carrying Place Trail' and plays an essential role in the region.

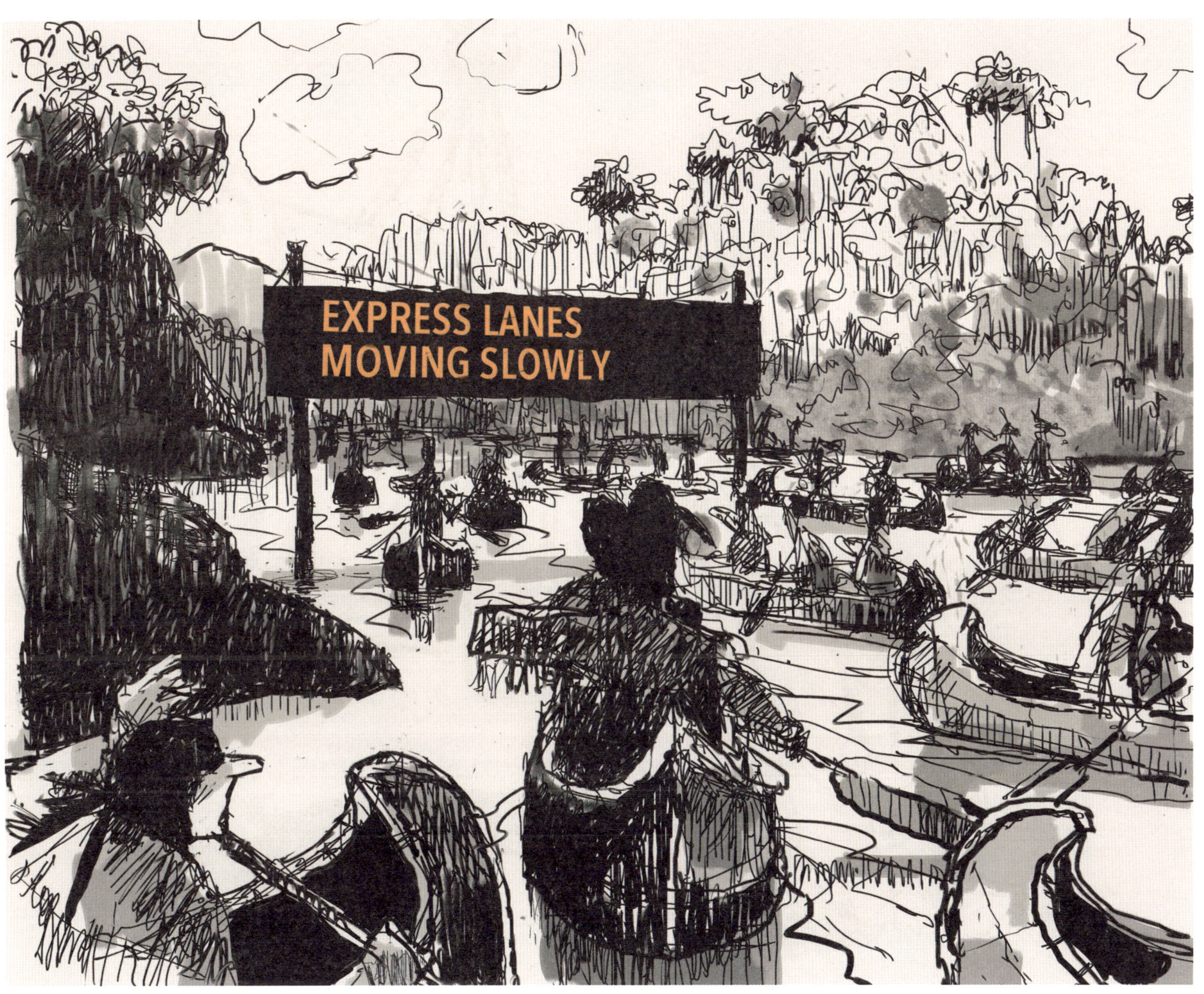
EXPRESS LANES
MOVING SLOWLY

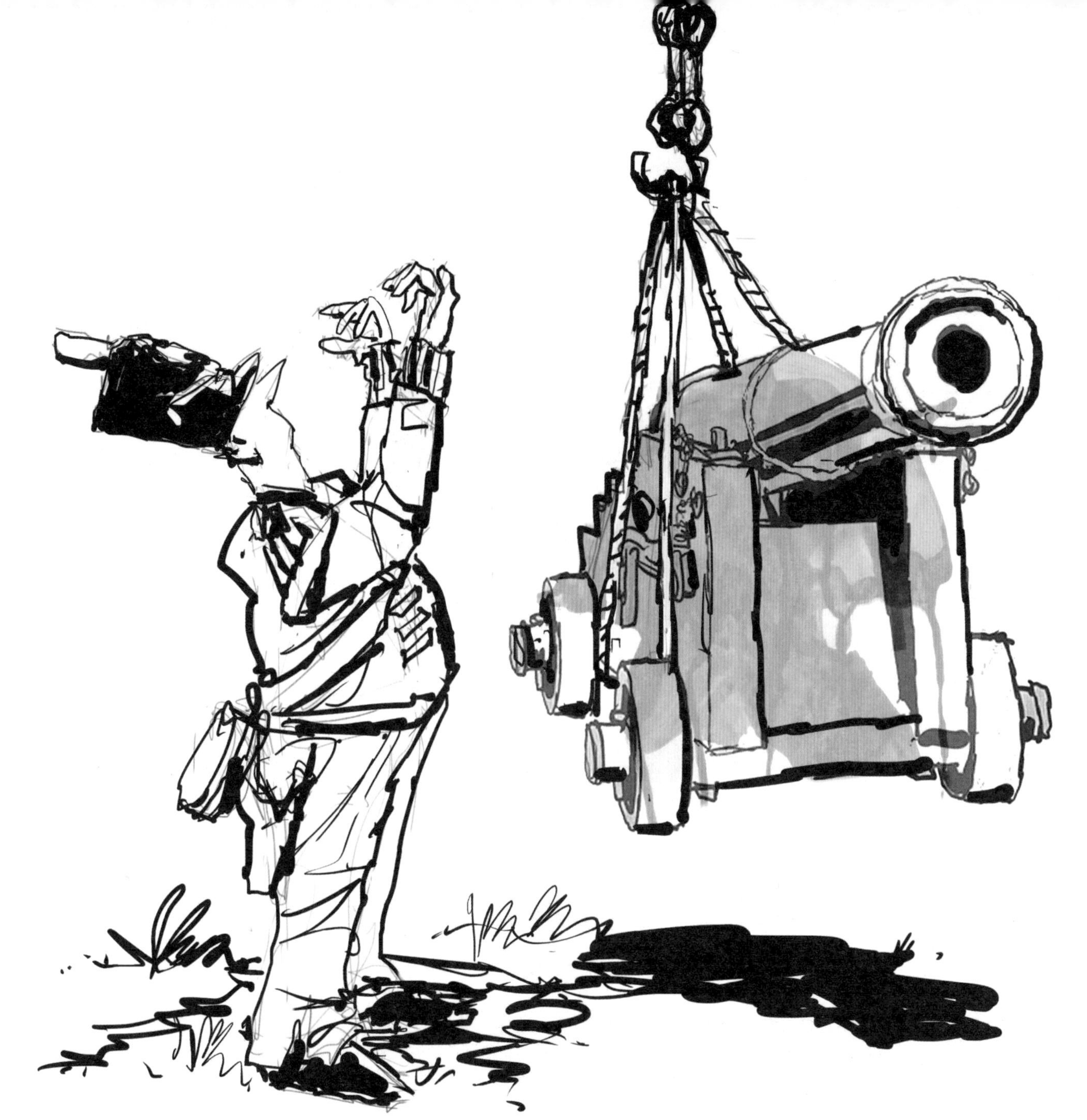

EUROPE ARRIVES ON THE SCENE

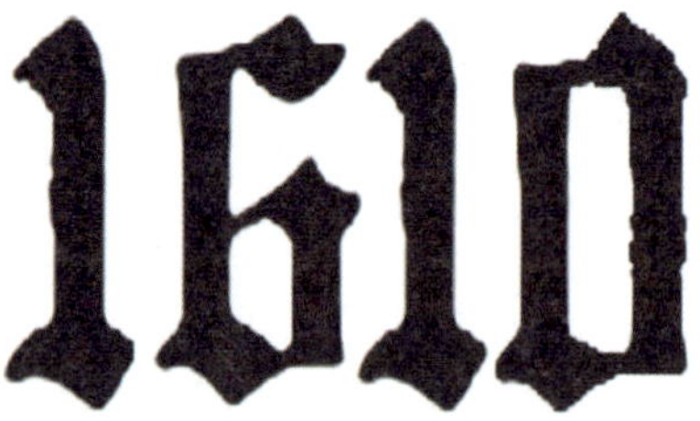

Étienne Brulé is dispatched from Quebec City by Samuel Champlain to explore The Great Lakes region. He is likely to have been the first European to visit this area. The geographical knowledge he brings back to Quebec City inspires expansion into the territory by French fur traders who establish trading posts in the area of present day Toronto. The first post was named Fort Douville and was constructed in 1720 in the Humber River area. A second post called Fort Pontneuf (also called Fort Toronto) was built in 1750. These trading posts were so successful that a third fort was constructed in 1751. The remains of that new post, Fort Rouillé, are marked by a plaque on the grounds of the Canadian National Exhibition, just west of Toronto's downtown core.

A French map from the late 1600s shows the lake, now known as Lake Simcoe, referred to as "Tarontos Lac".

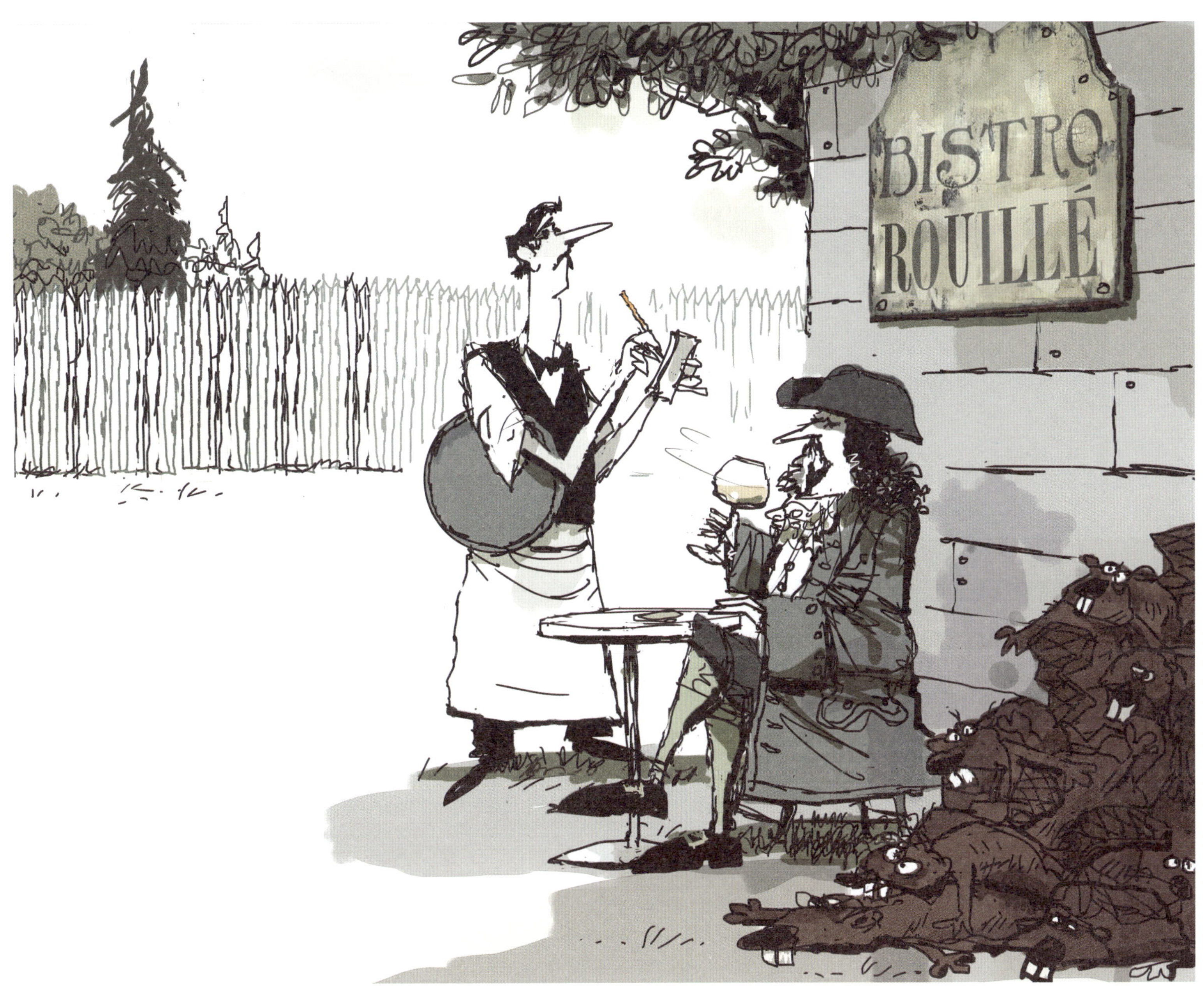
BISTRO
ROUILLÉ

THINGS BECOME INCREASINGLY COMPLICATED

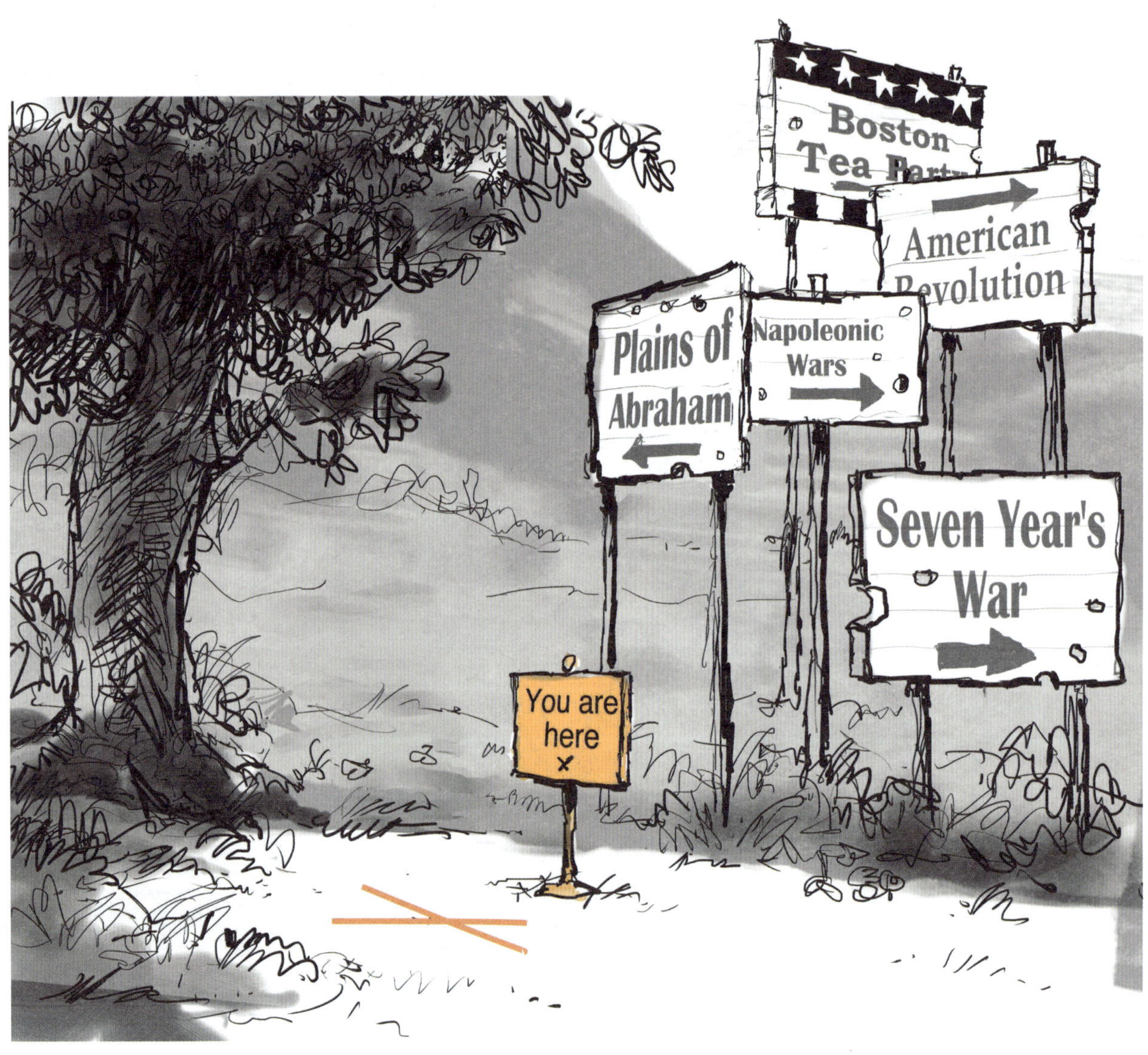

The Declaration of Independence in 1776 leads directly to the Revolutionary War, and ultimately the defeat of the British by the American colonists. Great Britain officially recognizes U.S.independence by signing the Treaty of Paris in 1783.

An officially recognized border running through the middle of the Great Lakes now divides the United States and the territory to the north, controlled by Great Britain.

Between 1783 and 1785, roughly 10,000 citizens who remain loyal to the Crown leave the United States and resettle in British North America.

1787

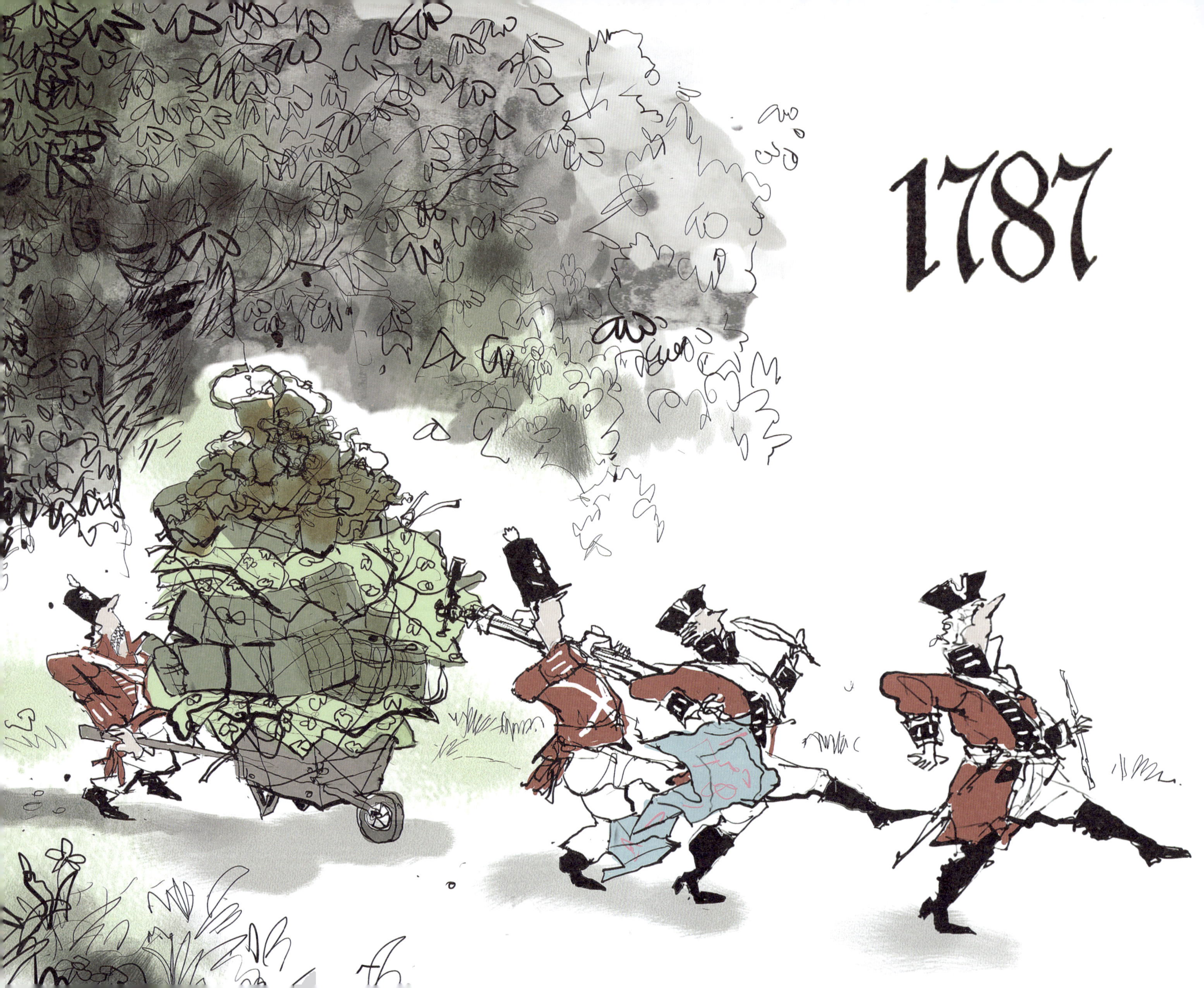

THE TORONTO PURCHASE

British-controlled territory close to the newly established border becomes increasingly strategically important.

The British undertake negotiations with First Nations leaders to purchase areas for the establishment of defensive positions and settlement locations for the newly arriving loyalists.

The area now occupied by the city of Toronto is purchased from the Mississaugas of New Credit for “some” money, 2,000 gun flints, 24 brass kettles, 120 mirrors, 24 laced hats, a bale of flowered flannel cloth and 96 gallons of rum.

The details of this transaction are questioned by the First Nations signatories and in 1805 the terms are renegotiated. This does not ultimately resolve the concerns.

In 2010, Canada agrees to pay $145 million for the land. This figure is determined by calculating the equivalent 1787 funds into current dollars.

1793

Deteriorating relations between the British and the United States of America during the late eighteenth century require the relocation of the capital of Upper Canada from its location at Niagara-on-the-Lake (then called 'Newark') to a safer area, further away from the United States border.

Upper Canada's lieutenant governor, John Graves Simcoe, decides to establish the new settlement in the area of today's London, Ontario.

His first choice is vetoed, and Simcoe goes with his second option. The new location has a natural protected harbour area between the Humber and the Don rivers, flowing into Lake Ontario, and presents an ideal spot to base a British fleet to control the lake.

Construction commences in 1793.

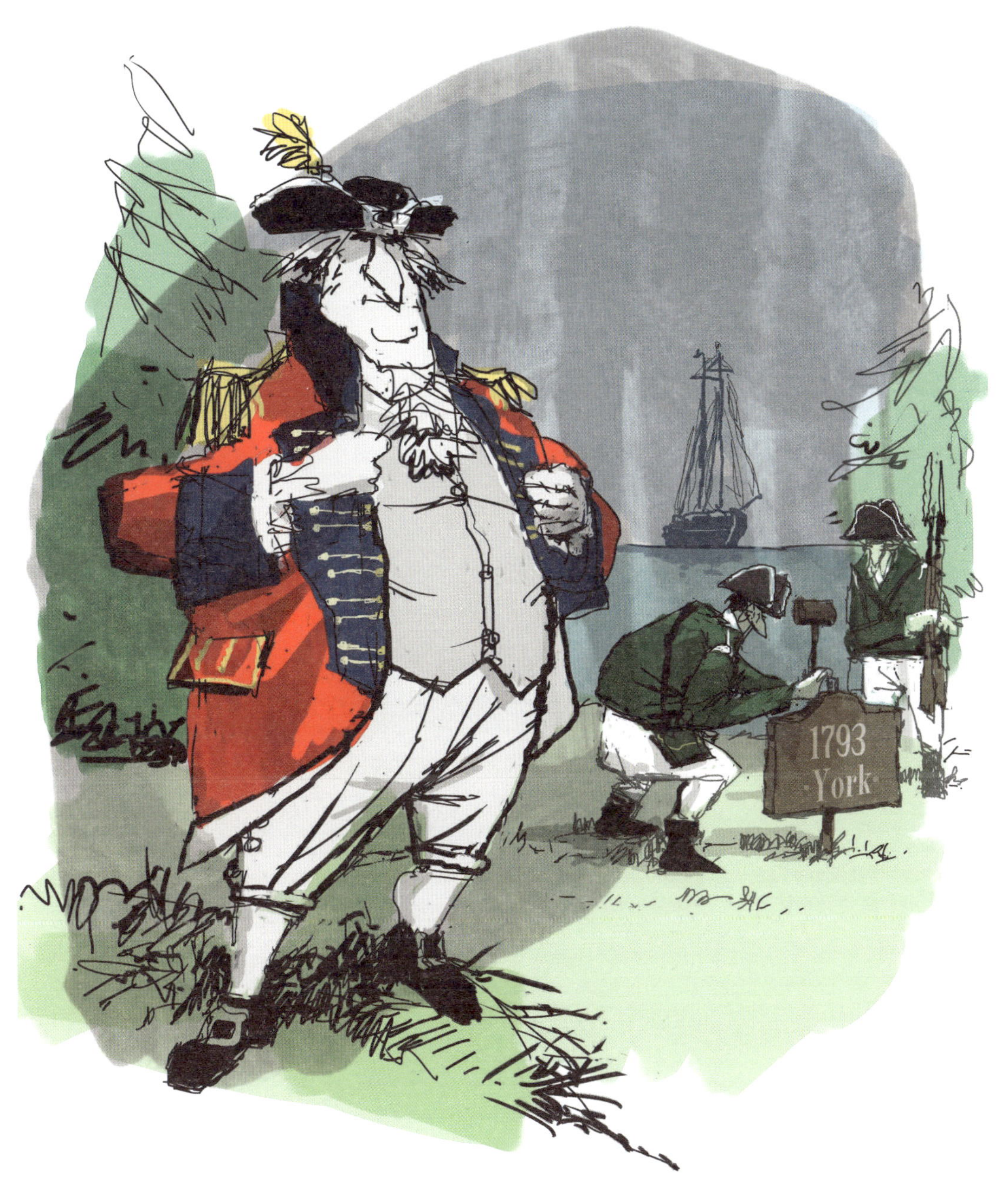
1793
·York·

Governor Simcoe names the site "Fort York"
after King George III's second son,
Frederick, Duke of York.

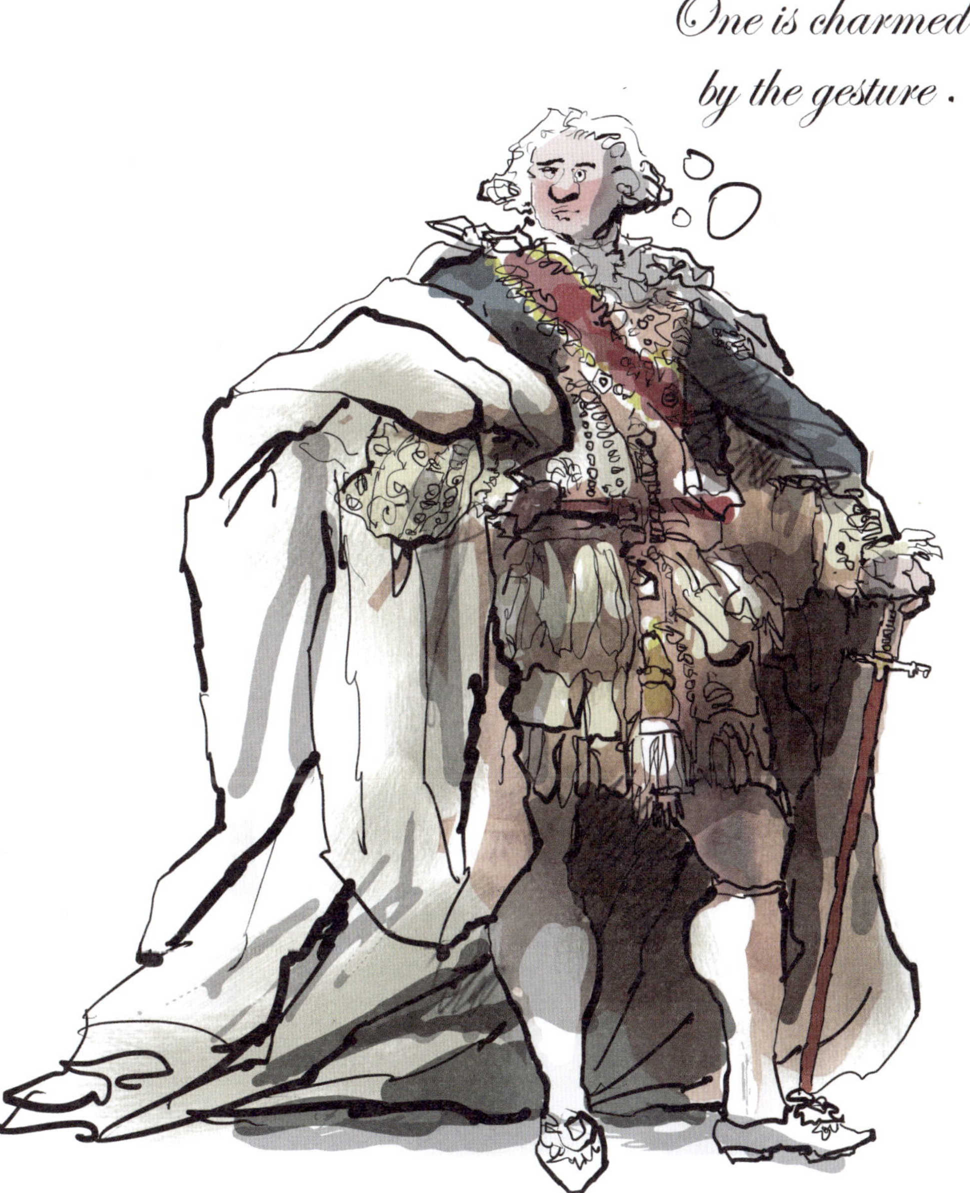

DUKE OF YORK.
(1763–1827)

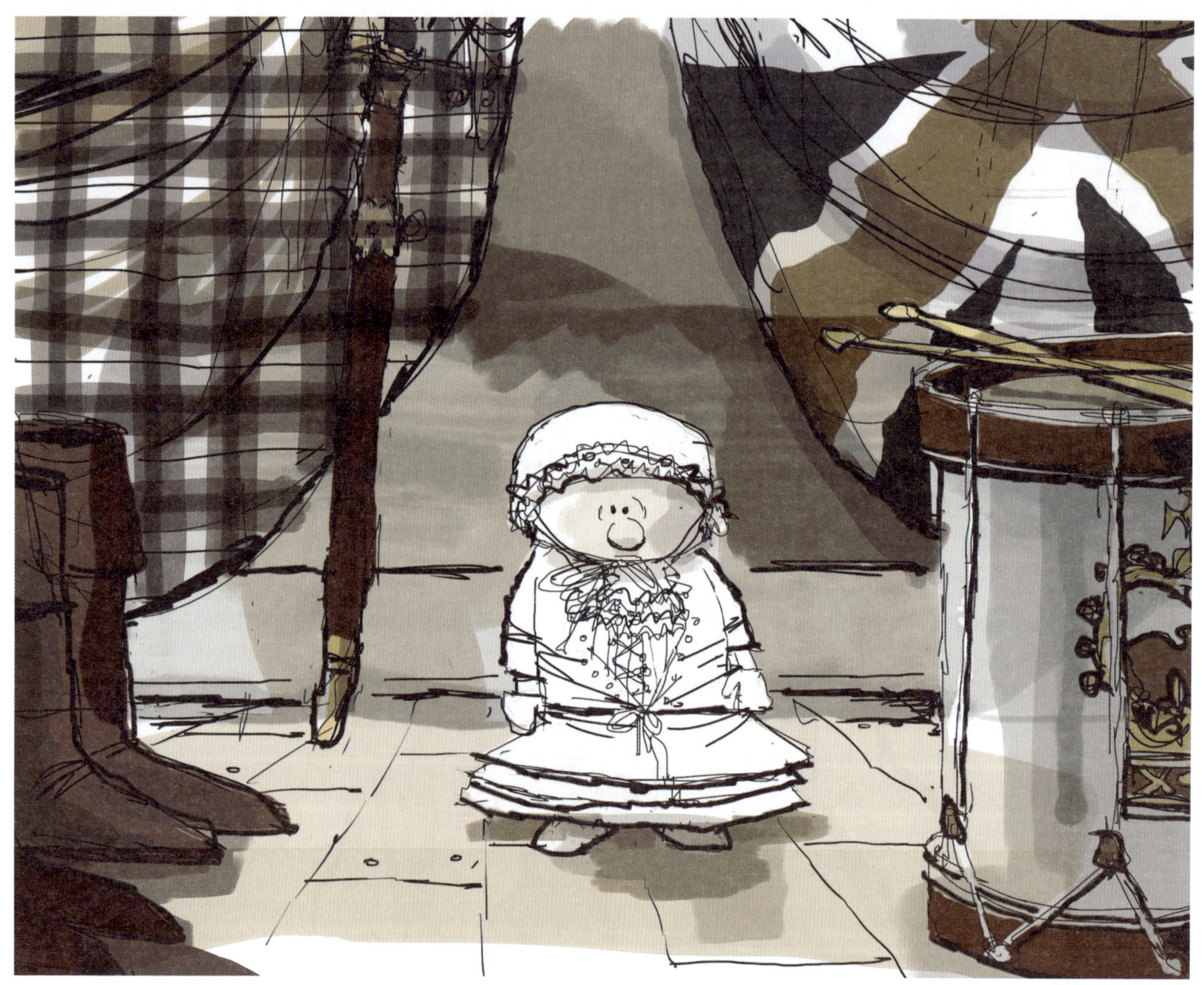

Garrison life is disciplined and spartan.

A small settlement begins growing to the east of the fort, near the lake shore. Civilian life is strongly influenced by military life in the garrison.

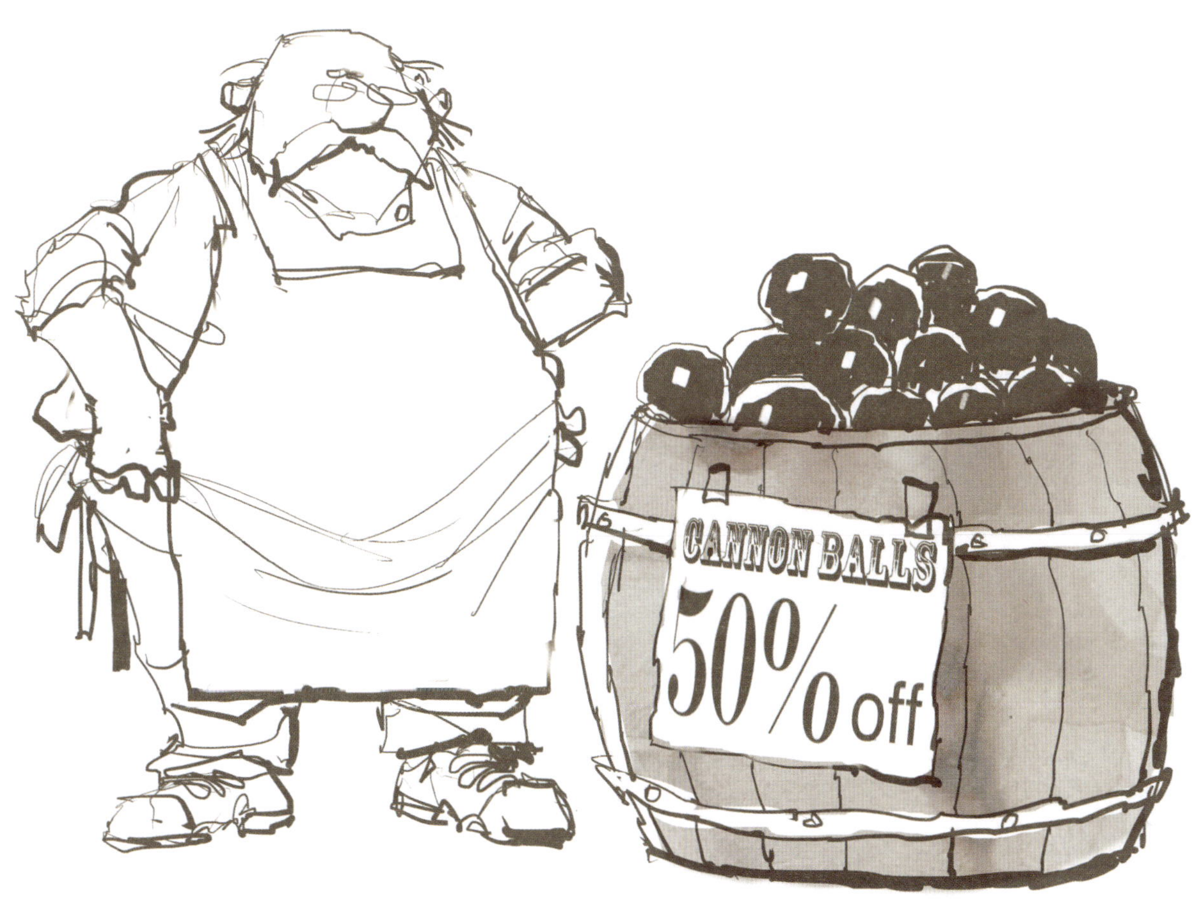

Elizabeth Simcoe, diarist, painter and wife of Governor Simcoe keeps a fascinating diary recording life in the emerging settlement. She also sketches and paints aspects of both garrison life and the wilderness flora and fauna around her.

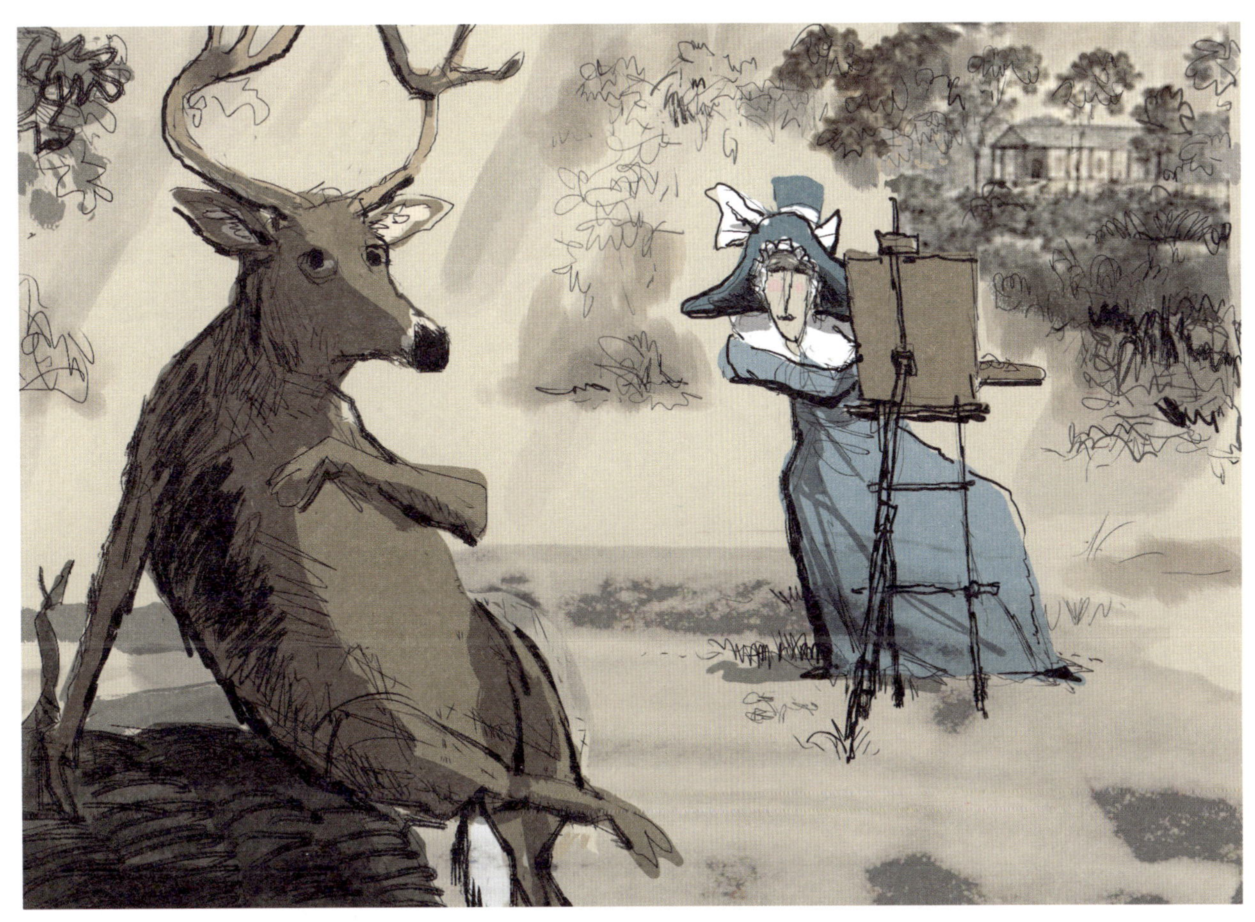

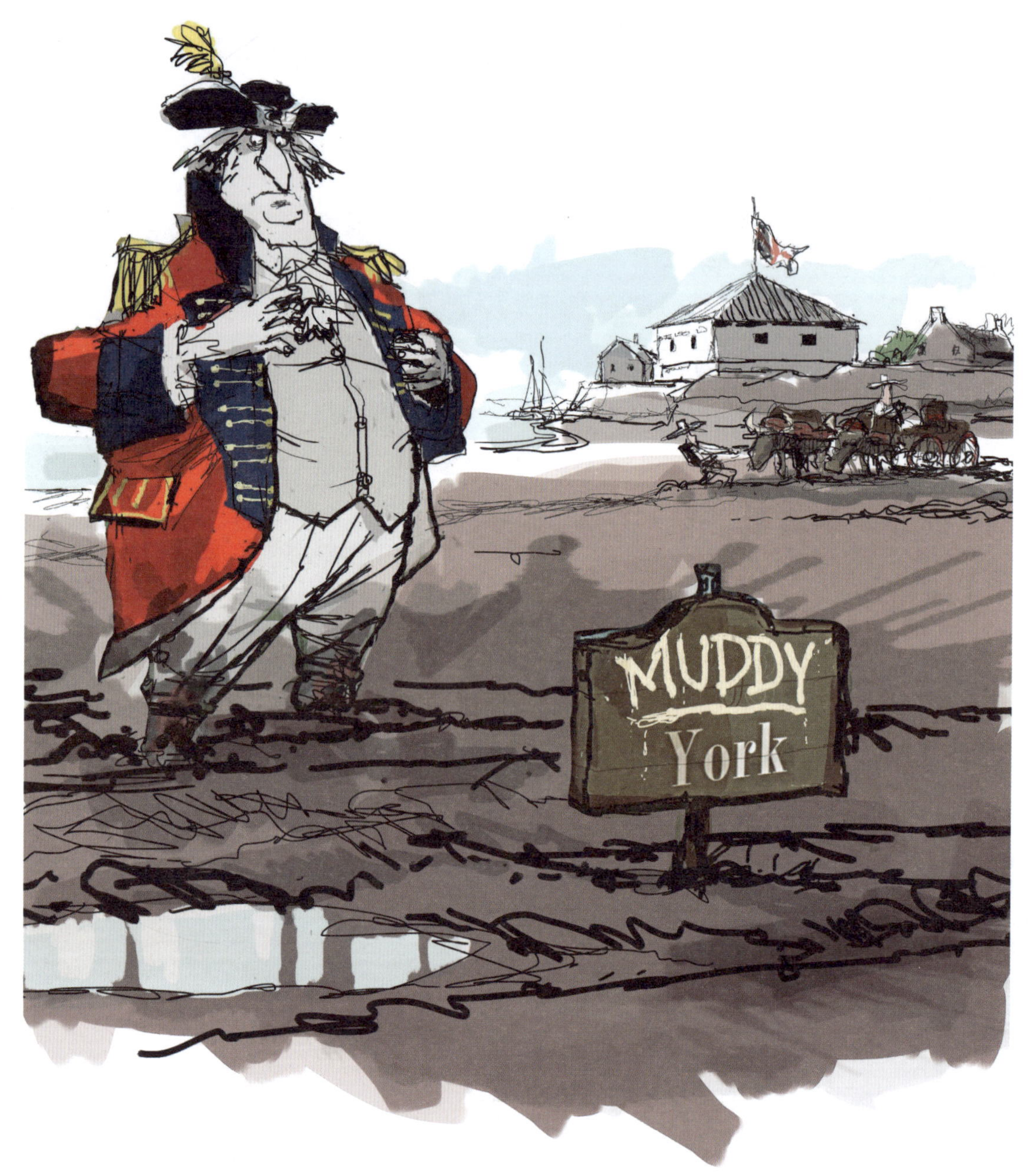
MUDDY
York

1796

Simcoe and his wife return to England.

A distinguishing feature of the new settlement provides its first nickname.

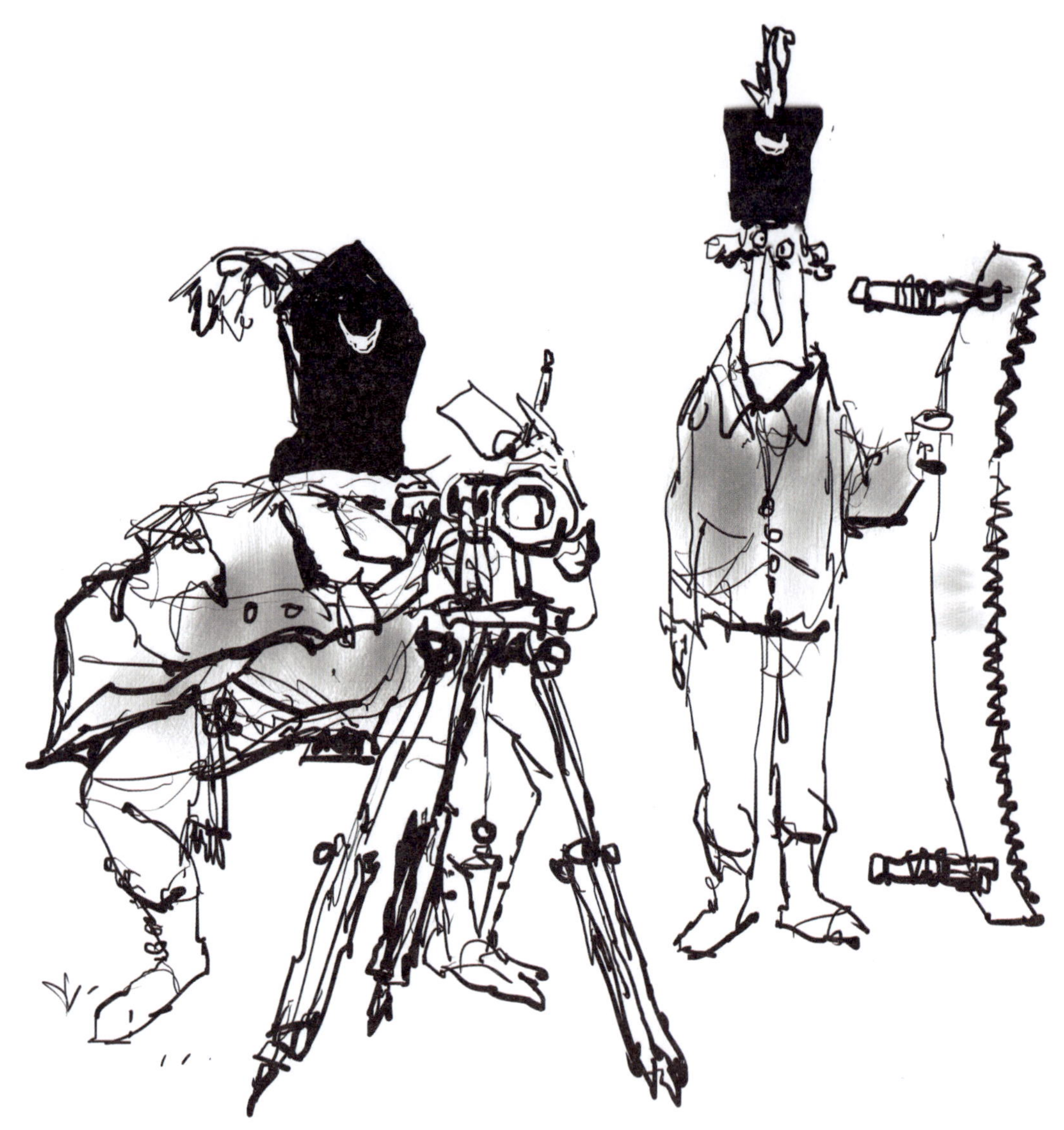

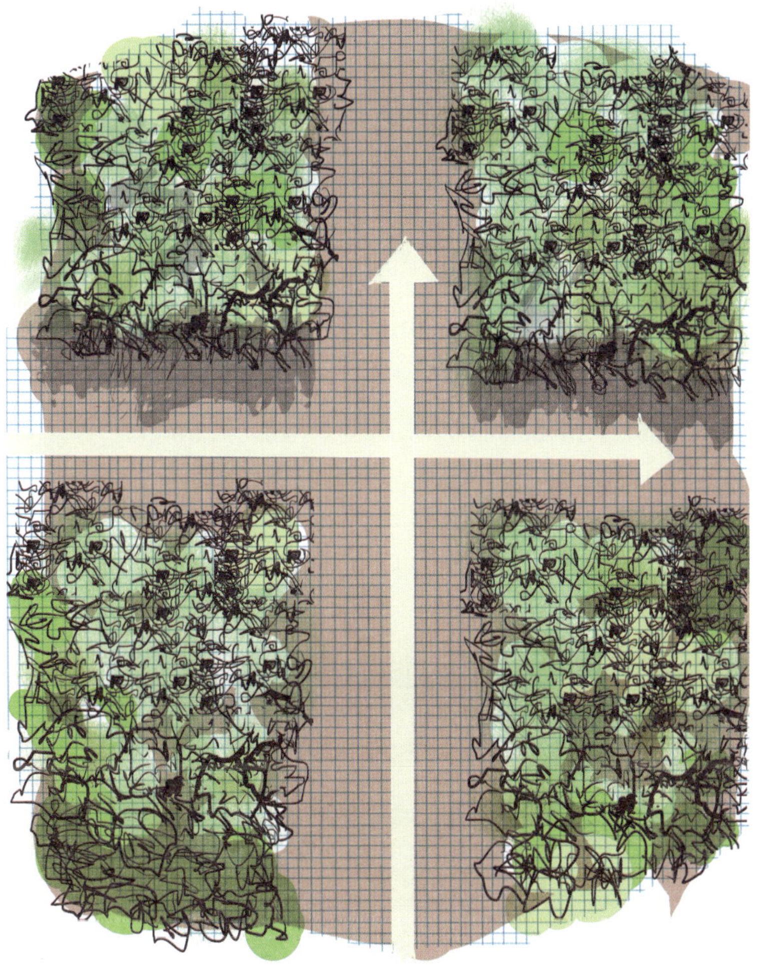

Streets in the newly emerging community, east of the fort, are cut through the forest and laid out in an uncompromising strict military grid which still defines the city's layout.

The War of 1812

Relations between Britain and the United States of America quickly deteriorate, and on June 18, 1812 war is officially declared.

In April of 1813, 2700 American troops land on the beaches near Fort York and quickly overpower the 750 defenders. The British abandon the fort and retreat towards the east. They set the powder magazine alight so that it doesn't fall into the hands of the Americans. The ensuing explosion kills or wounds over 200 Americans. The enraged survivors sack and burn the fort and the settlement around it.

The scope of this destruction enrages the British who burn Washington D.C. in 1814 in an act of revenge.

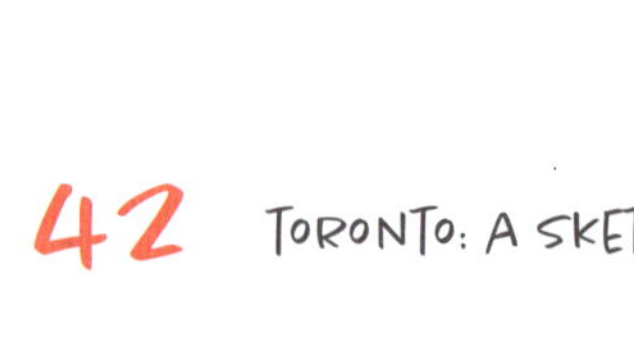

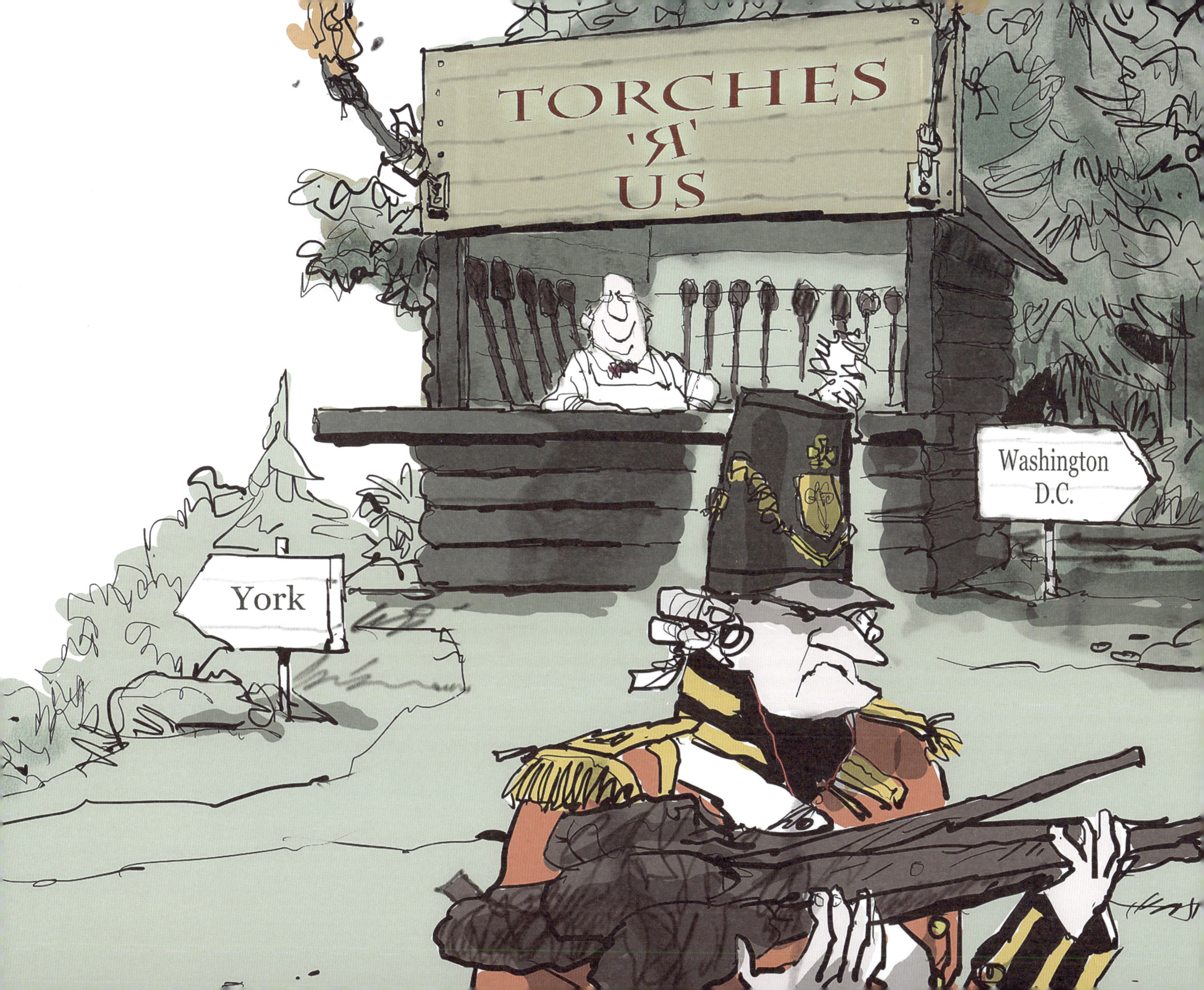
TORCHES
'Я'
US
Washington
D.C.
York

1814

The war reaches a stalemate with no conclusive victor.
A treaty is signed in Ghent, Belgium on December 24, 1814.
Repairs and new construction recommences in
Upper Canada's community of York.

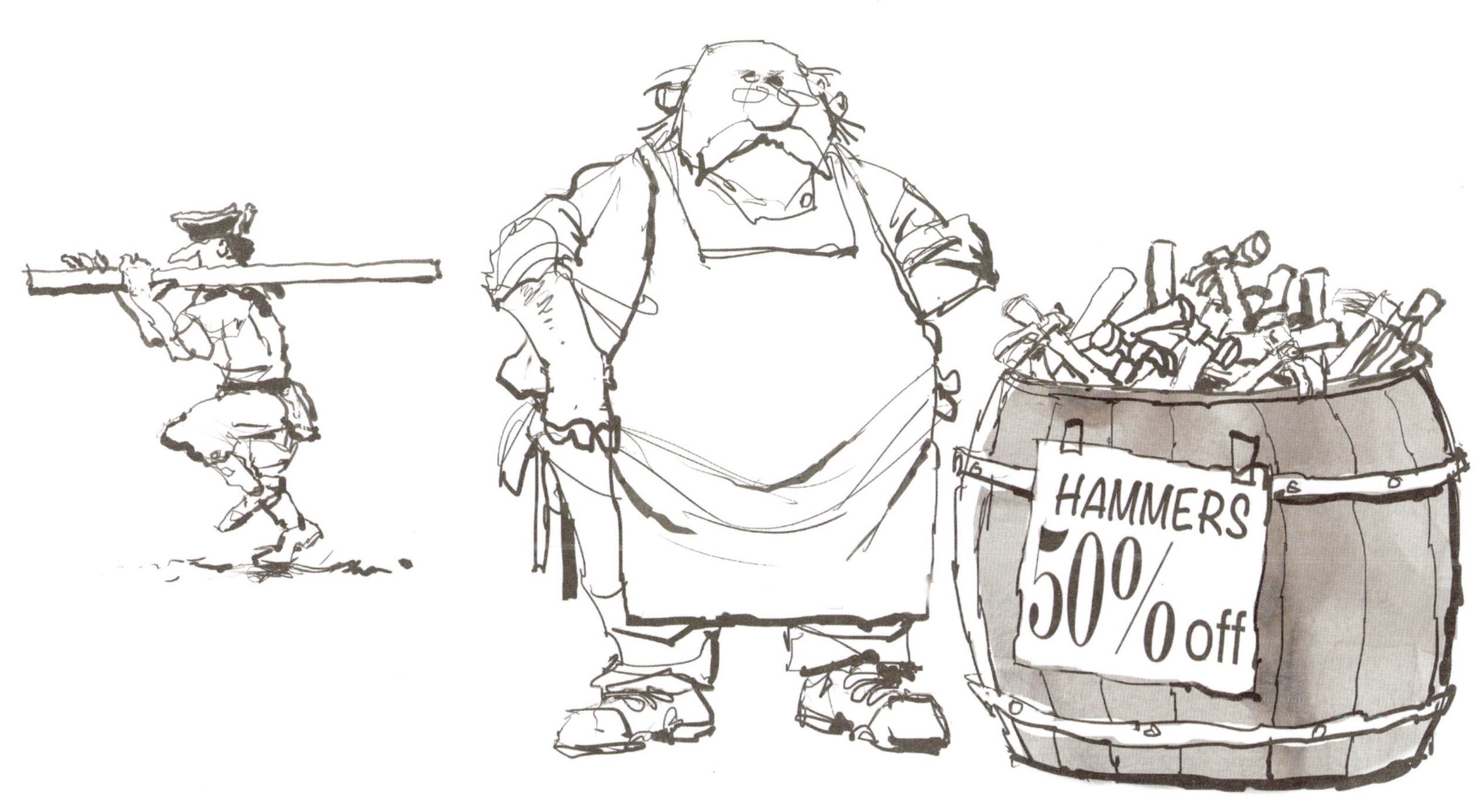
HAMMERS
50% off

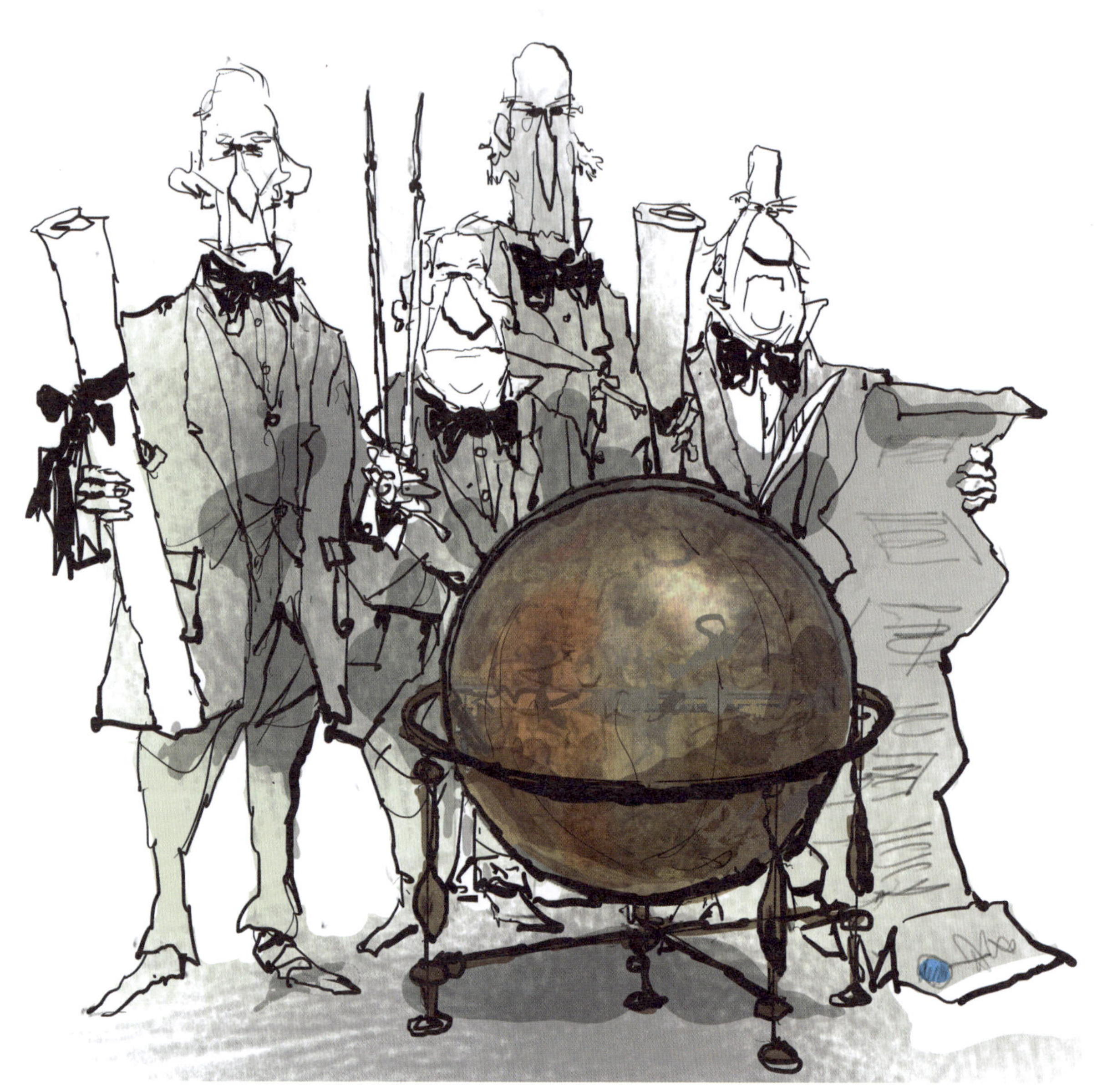

1820

THE FAMILY COMPACT

In contrast to the newly established republican form of government to the south of them, The British administration in Upper Canada wishes to maintain a more traditional system of authority, one loyal to the Crown.

A small group of appointed officials assumes the task of governing the province. Anglican Bishop, John Strachan, is one of the most well known of the small group.

Lands are surveyed and allotted, in many cases to friends and associates of the Family Compact. This body of closely tied elites is anxious to establish an infrastructure of industry, transportation and banking.

The Anglican Church receives 1/7 of all Crown Land. Other faiths begin to challenge this system of privilege.

1834

The thriving village of York has surpassed 9,000 inhabitants. Even in these early days it is quickly evolving into a financial centre for the surrounding agricultural communities. On March 6, 1834 the unincorporated town of York transforms into the incorporated City of Toronto.

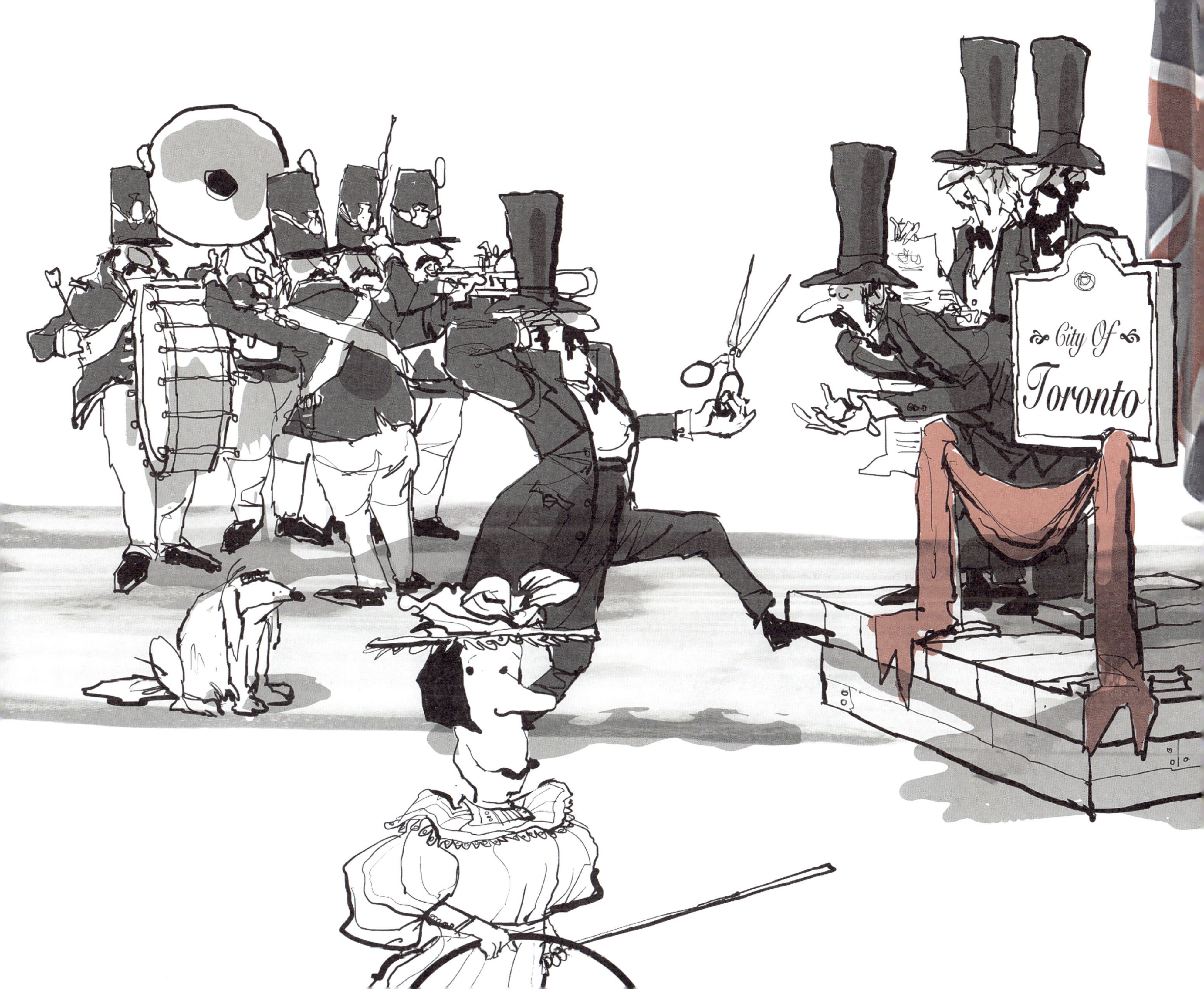
City Of
Toronto

1837

THE UPPER CANADA REBELLION

Revolution is in the air.

The American Revolution of 1776, the French Revolution, the Irish Rebellion of 1798, and the Haitian Revolution ending in 1804 are all recent memories. In November of 1837, Lower Canada (now Quebec) breaks out in rebellion against the British Crown.

A month later, in Toronto, an armed militia under the leadership of William Lyon Mackenzie confronts government forces. Their goal is to overthrow the existing regime and replace it with what they see as a more open form of government.

The rebels are unsuccessful, yet many of the reforms they were proposing are ultimately enacted in the colony as the power of the Family Compact continues to recede.

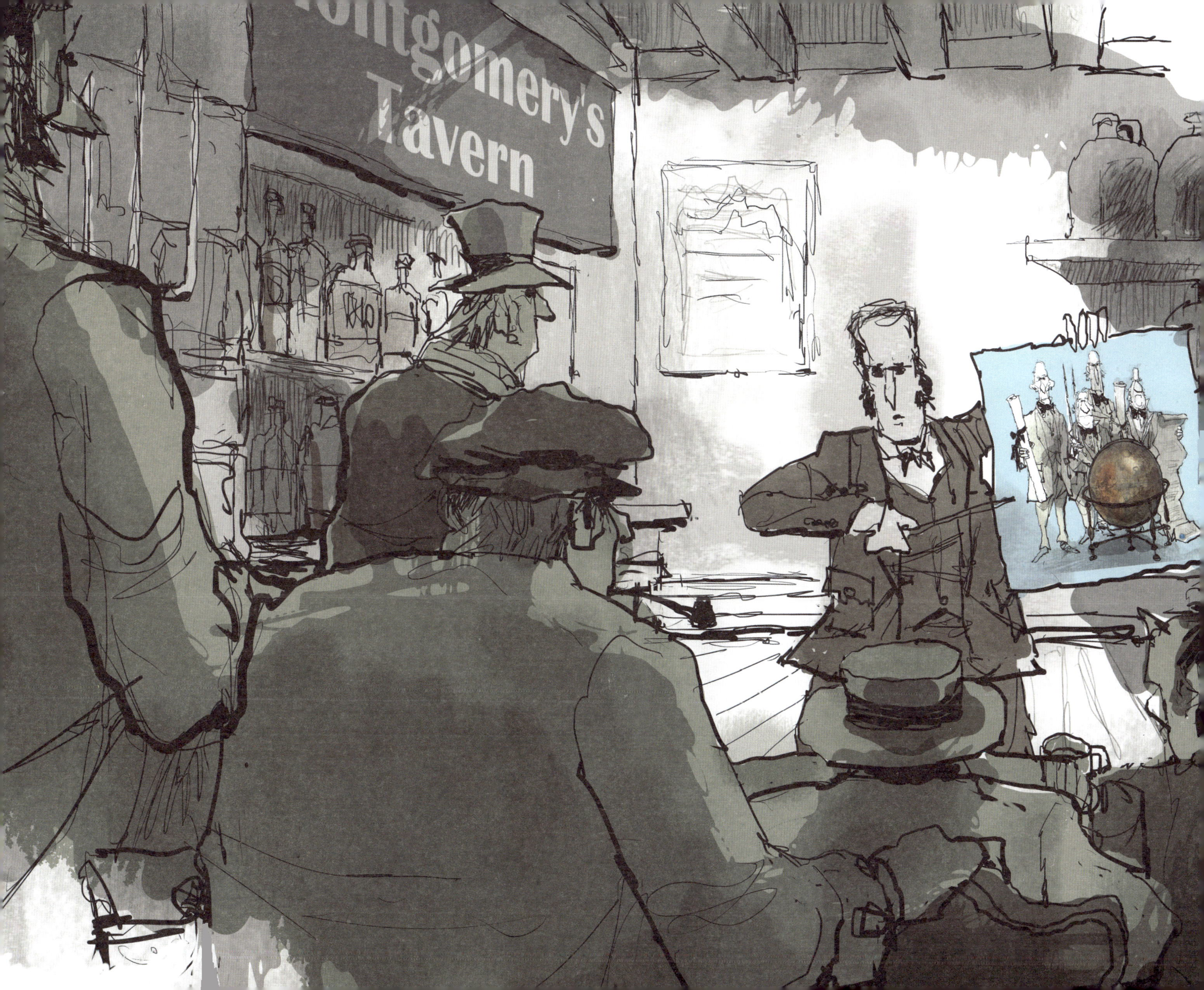
ontgomery's
Tavern

1845

In 1845, the Legislature of Canada passes the "Sunday Observance Act" to prevent the "profanation of the Lord's Day".

Toronto enthusiastically complies.

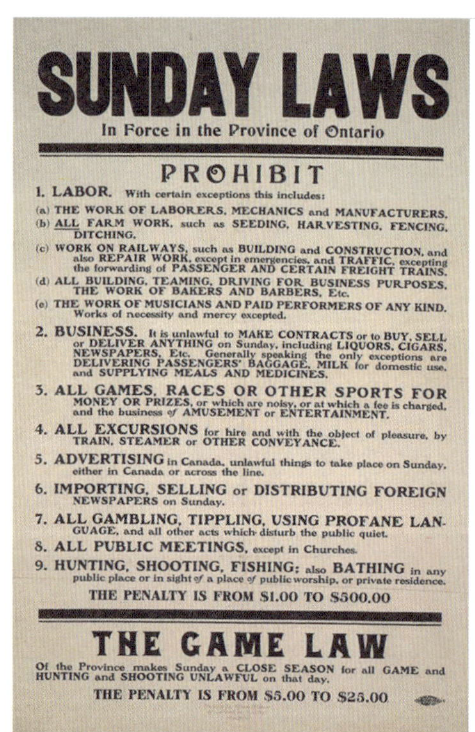

SUNDAY LAWS

In Force in the Province of Ontario

PROHIBIT

1. LABOR. With certain exceptions this includes:

(a) THE WORK OF LABORERS, MECHANICS and MANUFACTURERS.

(b) ALL FARM WORK, such as SEEDING, HARVESTING, FENCING, DITCHING.

(c) WORK ON RAILWAYS, such as BUILDING and CONSTRUCTION, and also REPAIR WORK, except in emergencies, and TRAFFIC, excepting the forwarding of PASSENGER AND CERTAIN FREIGHT TRAINS.

(d) ALL BUILDING, TEAMING, DRIVING FOR BUSINESS PURPOSES, THE WORK OF BAKERS AND BARBERS, Etc.

(e) THE WORK OF MUSICIANS AND PAID PERFORMERS OF ANY KIND. Works of necessity and mercy excepted.

2. BUSINESS. It is unlawful to MAKE CONTRACTS or to BUY, SELL or DELIVER ANYTHING on Sunday, including LIQUORS, CIGARS, NEWSPAPERS, Etc. Generally speaking the only exceptions are DELIVERING PASSENGERS' BAGGAGE, MILK for domestic use, and SUPPLYING MEALS AND MEDICINES.

3. ALL GAMES, RACES OR OTHER SPORTS FOR MONEY OR PRIZES, or which are noisy, or at which a fee is charged, and the business of AMUSEMENT or ENTERTAINMENT.

4. ALL EXCURSIONS for hire and with the object of pleasure, by TRAIN, STEAMER or OTHER CONVEYANCE.

5. ADVERTISING in Canada, unlawful things to take place on Sunday, either in Canada or across the line.

6. IMPORTING, SELLING or DISTRIBUTING FOREIGN NEWSPAPERS on Sunday.

7. ALL GAMBLING, TIPPLING, USING PROFANE LANGUAGE, and all other acts which disturb the public quiet.

8. ALL PUBLIC MEETINGS, except in Churches.

9. HUNTING, SHOOTING, FISHING: also BATHING in any public place or in sight of a place of public worship, or private residence.

THE PENALTY IS FROM $1.00 TO $500.00

THE GAME LAW

Of the Province makes Sunday a CLOSE SEASON for all GAME and HUNTING and SHOOTING UNLAWFUL on that day.

THE PENALTY IS FROM $5.00 TO $25.00

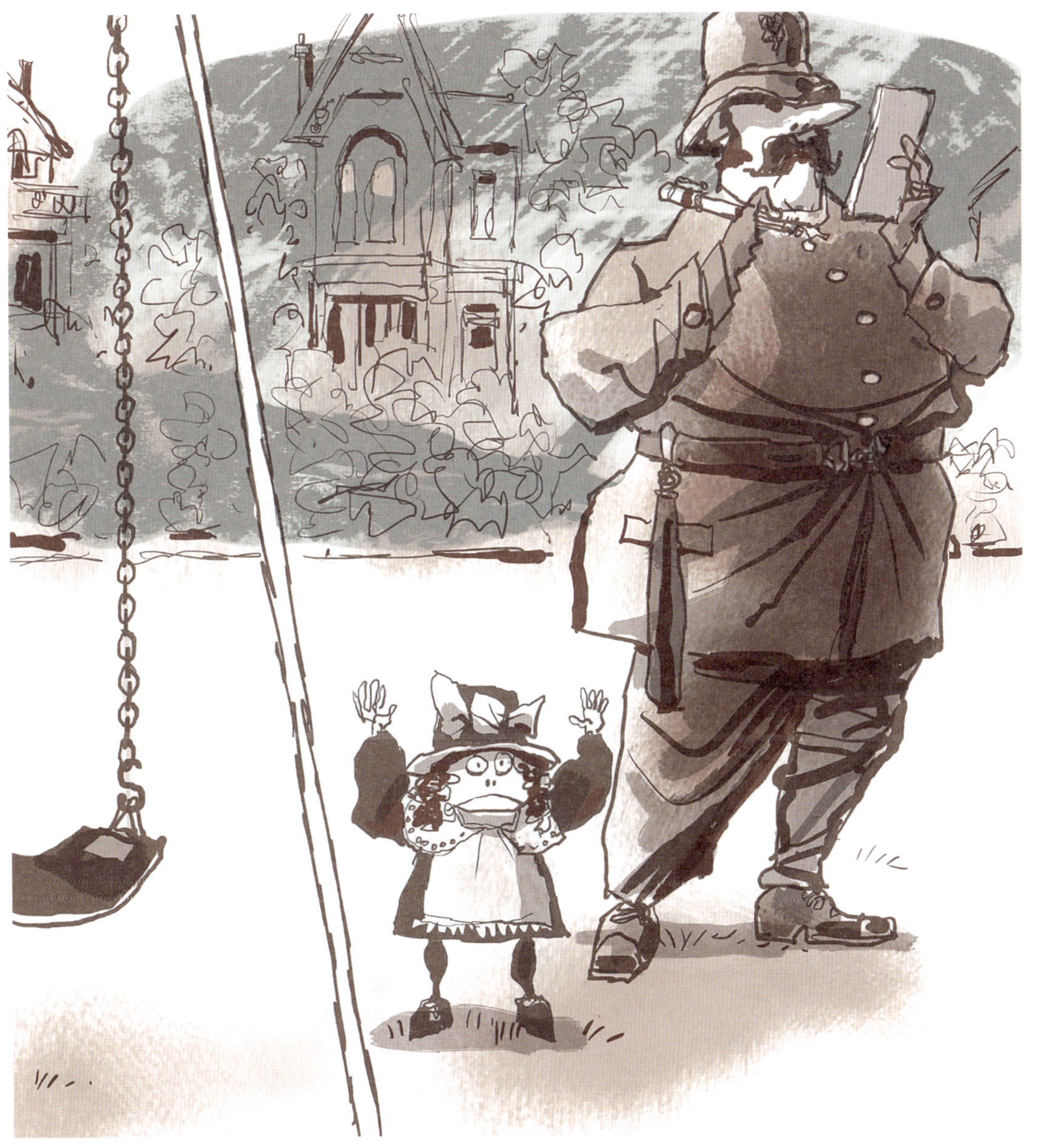

"It must be good to die in Toronto. The transition between life and death would be continuous, painless and scarcely noticeable in this silent town. I dreaded the Sundays and prayed to God that if he chose for me to die in Toronto, he would let it be on a Saturday afternoon to save me from one more Toronto Sunday."

Leopold Infeld

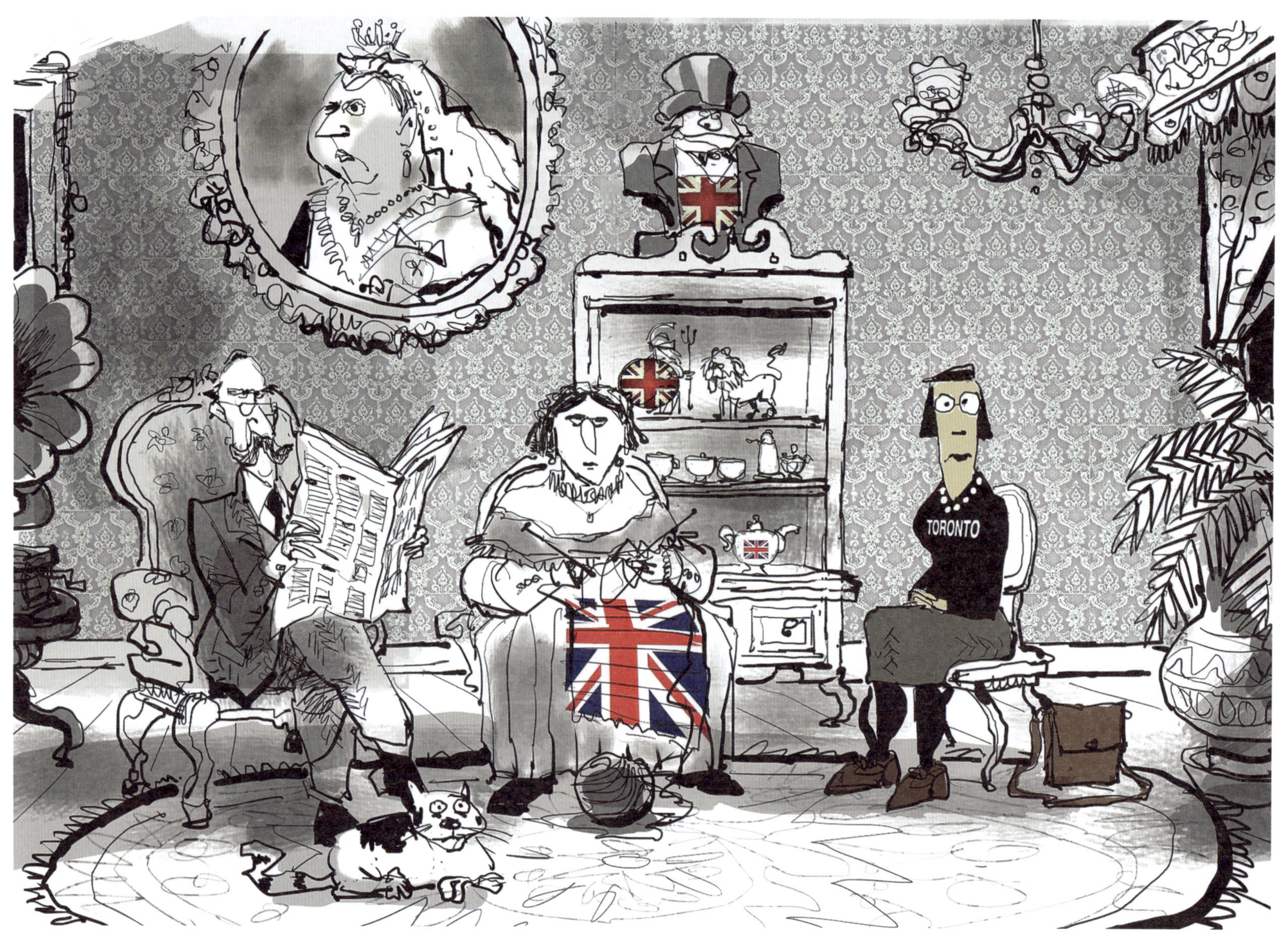
TORONTO

"CANADA-THE MOST PAROCHIAL NATIONETTE ON EARTH . . . I HAVE BEEN LIVING IN THIS SANCTIMONIOUS ICEBOX..PAINTING PORTRAITS OF THE OPULENT METHODISTS OF TORONTO. METHODISM AND MONEY IN THIS CITY HAVE PRODUCED A SORT OF HELL OF DULLNESS."

WYNDHAM LEWIS

1853

Rail transportation comes to Toronto.

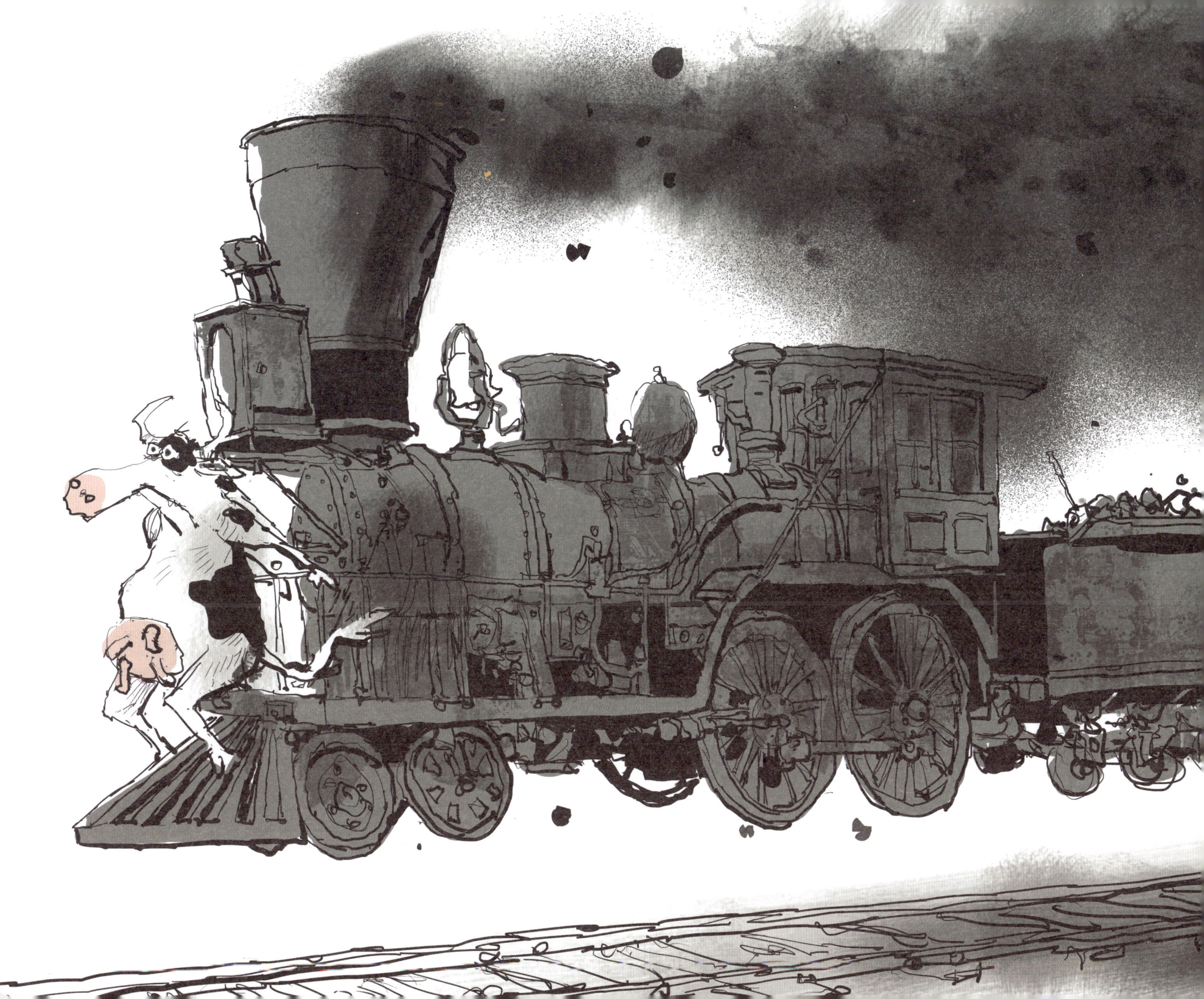

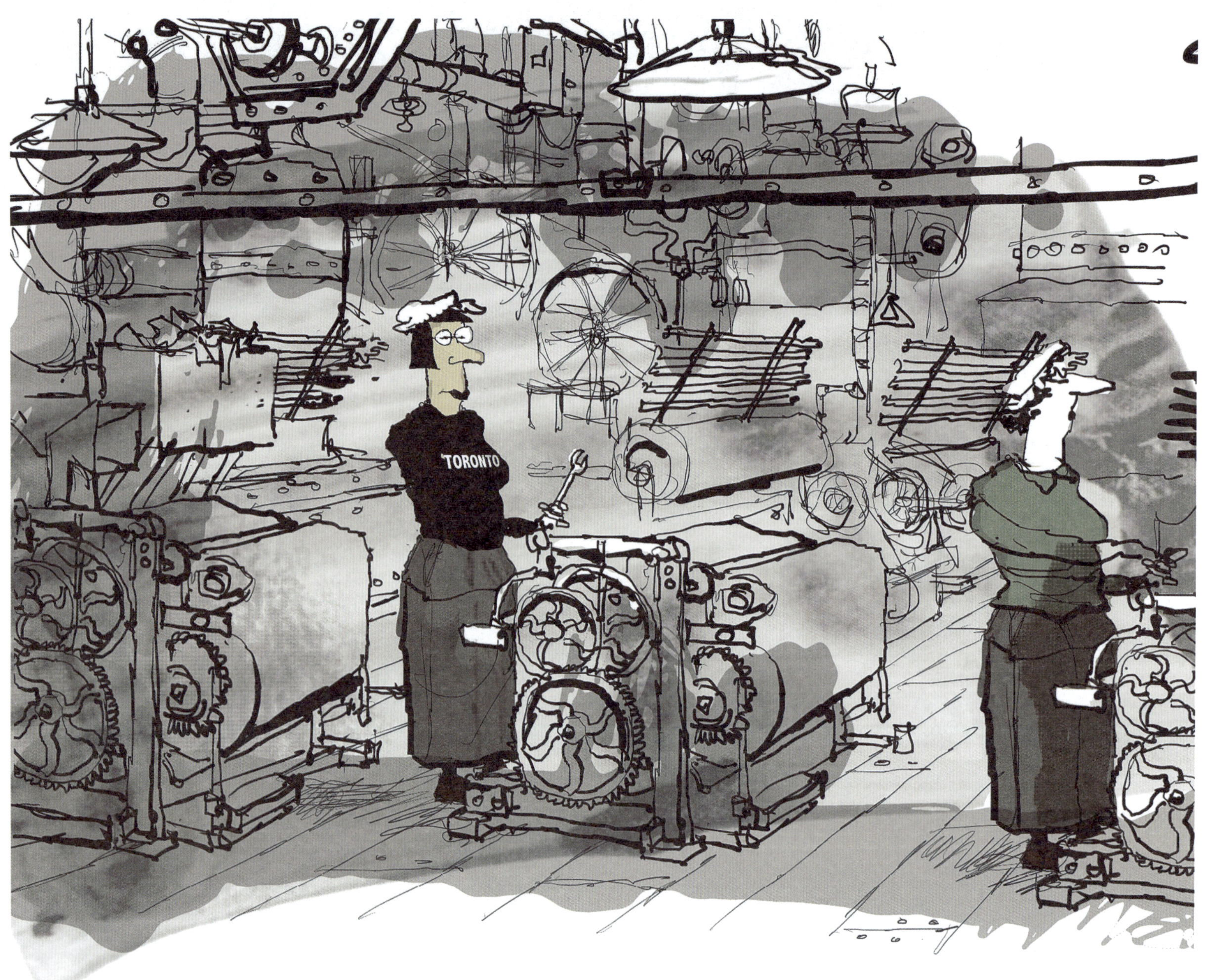
TORONTO

The arrival of the railroad boosts many sectors of the economy. Foundries, factories, breweries and distilleries are constructed at an increasing pace. Banking and retail industries thrive as a result of the new industrial activity.

As the city increasingly becomes a flourishing financial centre, lavish banks are constructed, often in a popular style known as "Greek Revival".

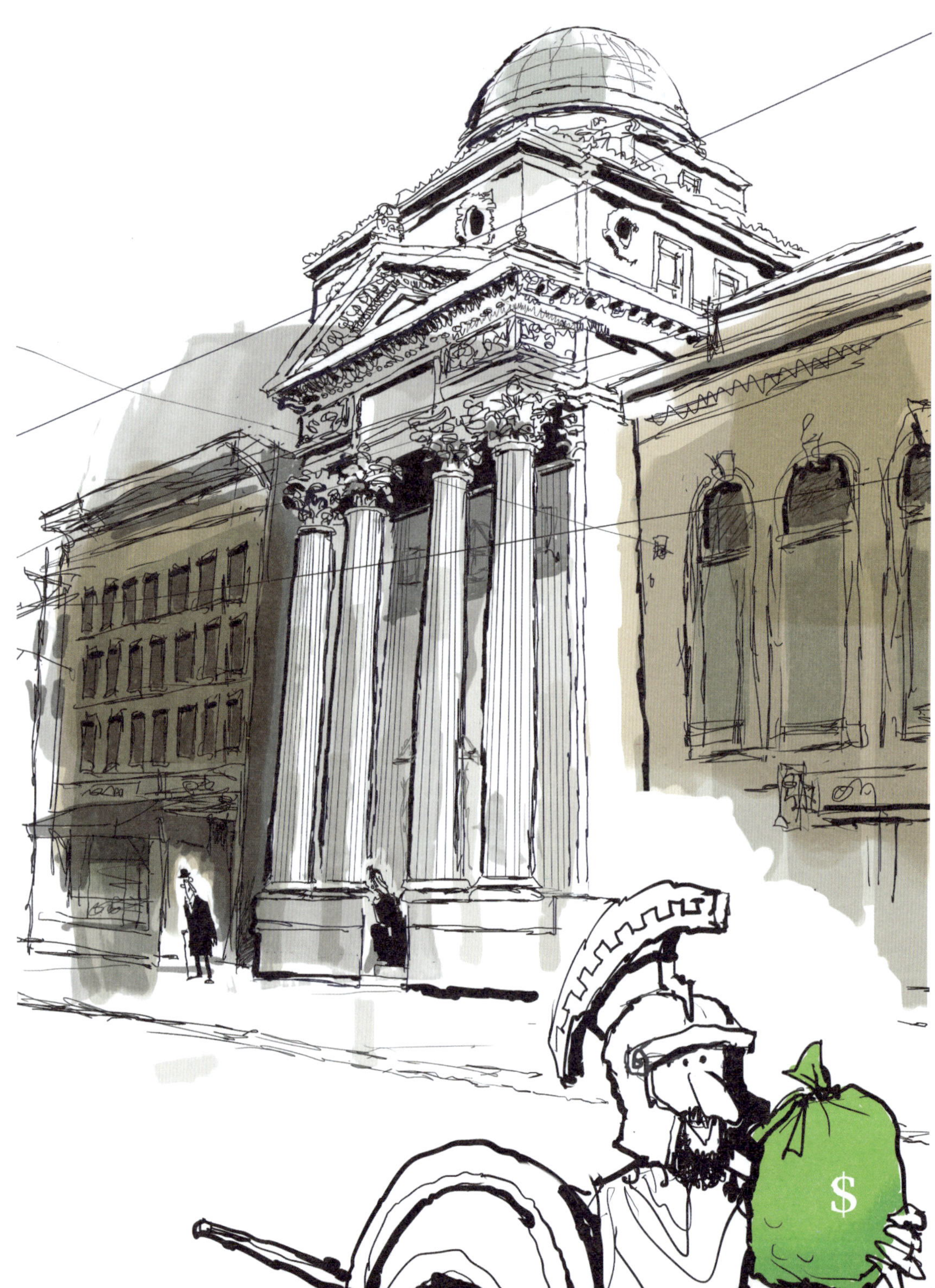

The late 1860s sees the establishment of the immensely successful Eaton's retail business, which would grow into a nation-wide chain lasting over a century.

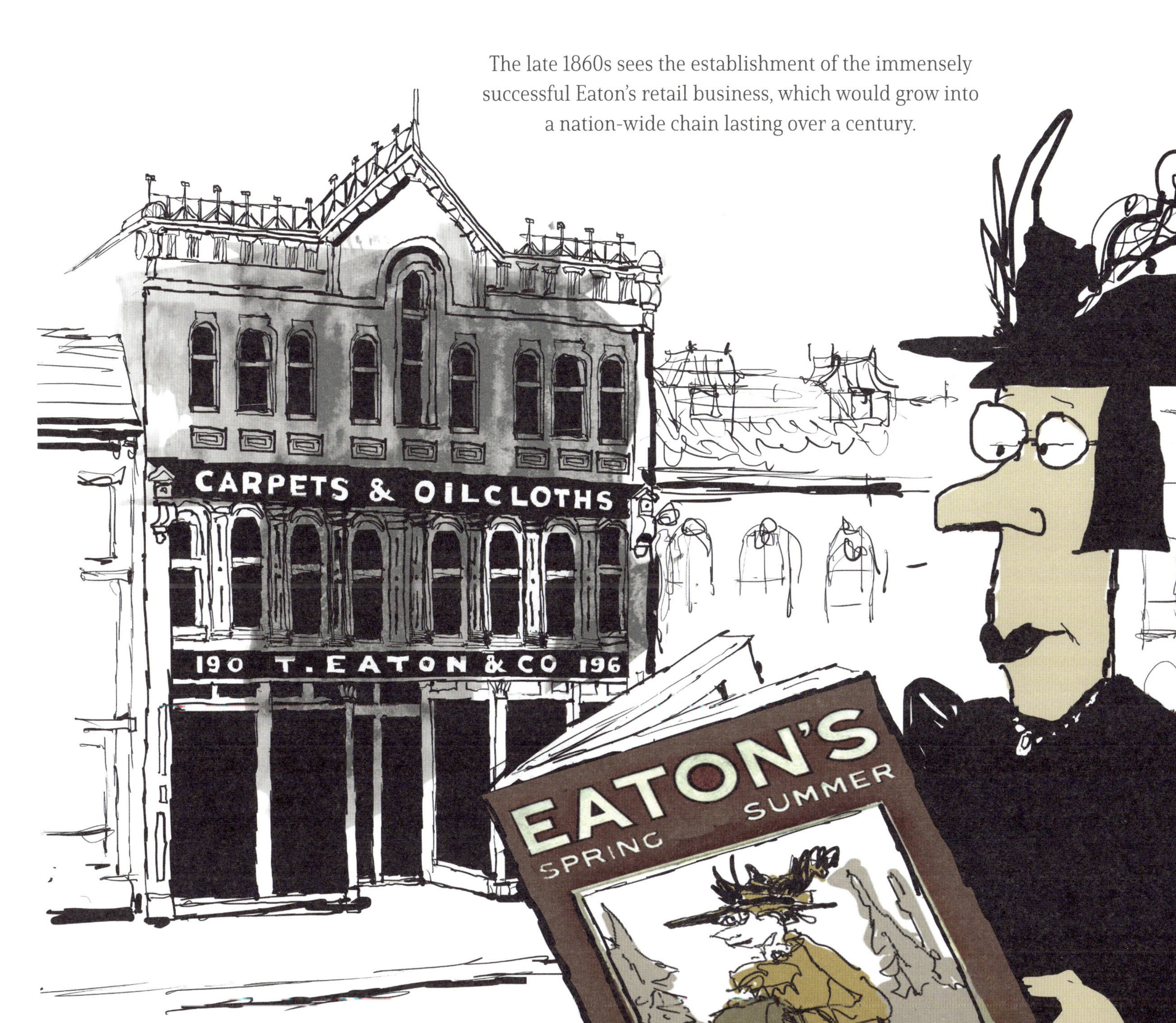

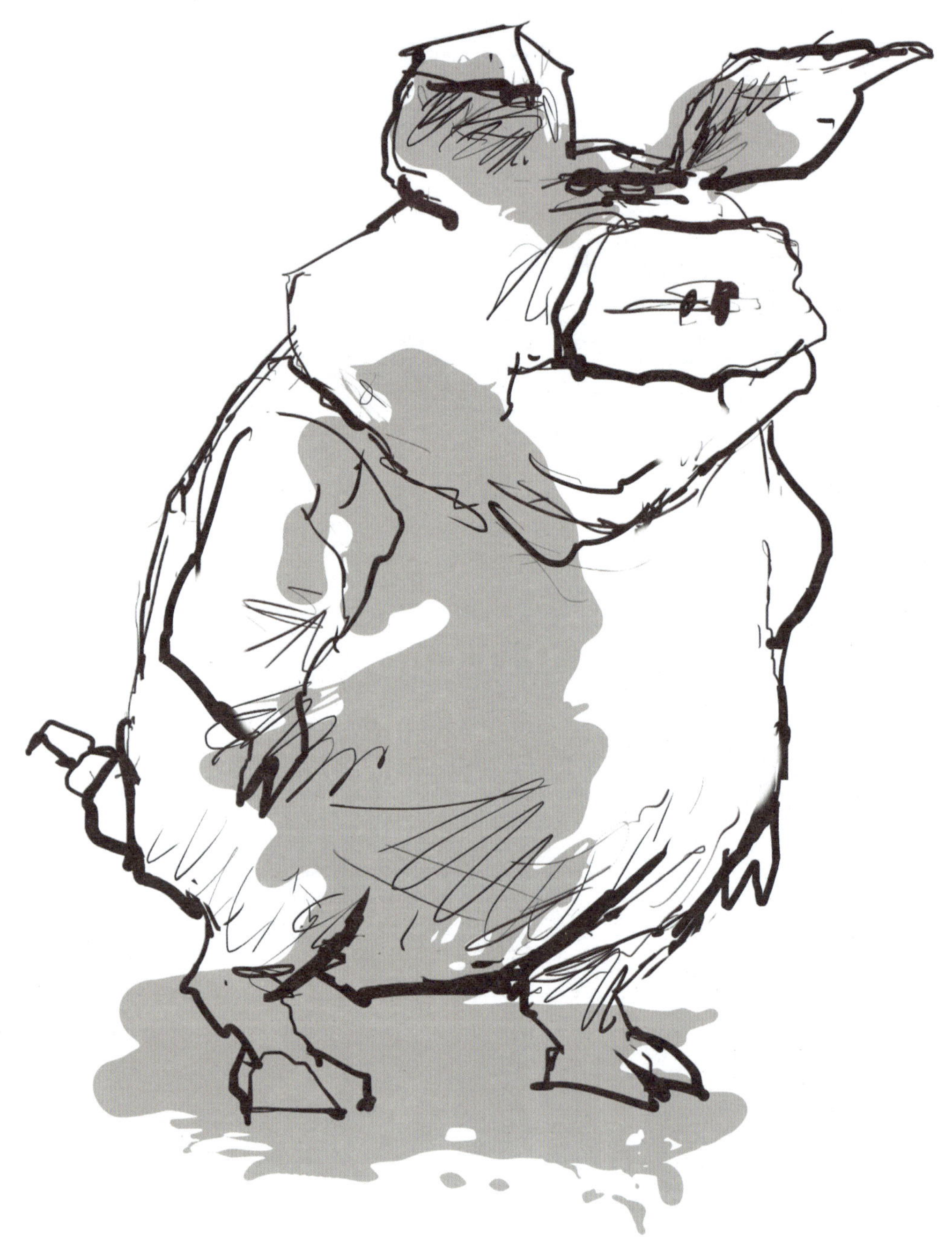

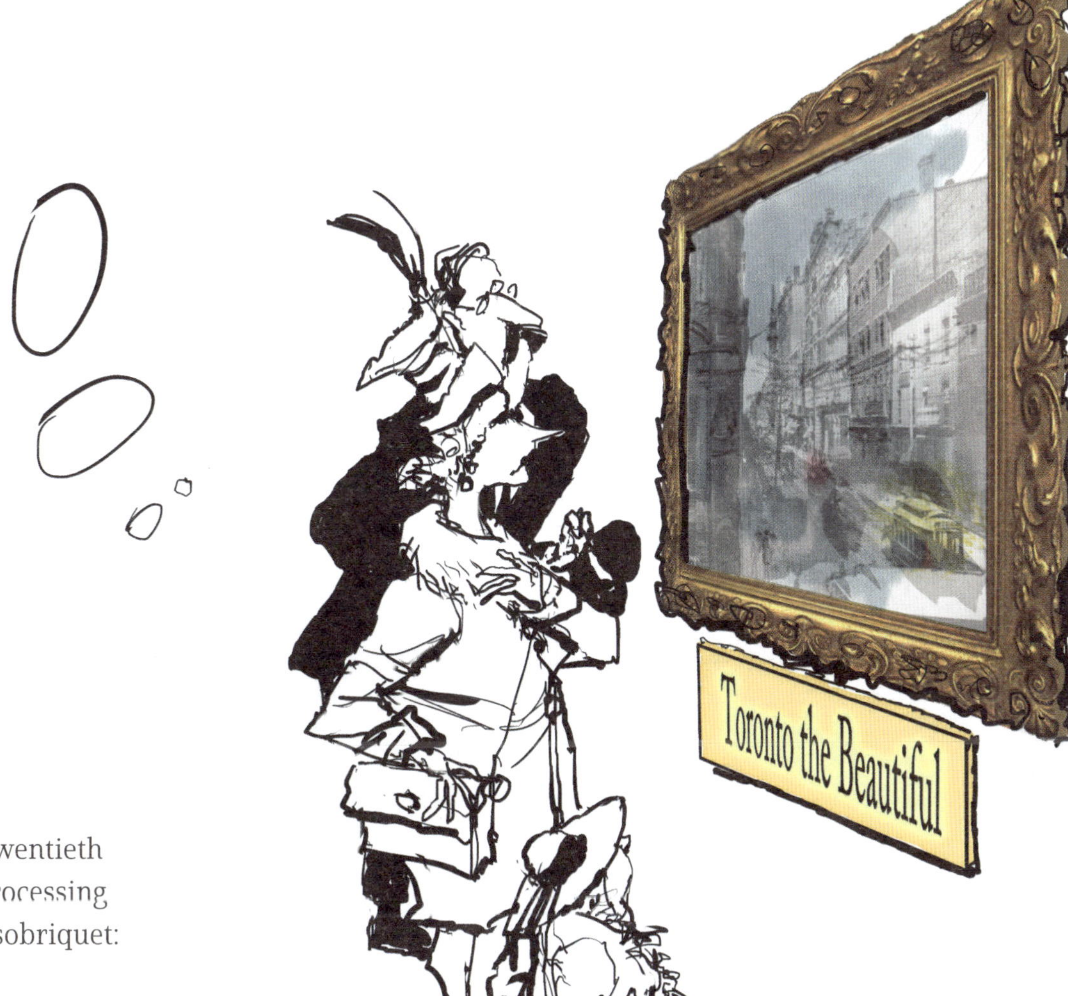

In the late nineteenth century and early twentieth century Toronto becomes a major pork processing centre, which leads to its next endearing sobriquet:

"Hogtown."

Some observers contend that the "Hogtown" label reflects the response many people experience when contemplating the city.

1899

Toronto's new city hall is opened.

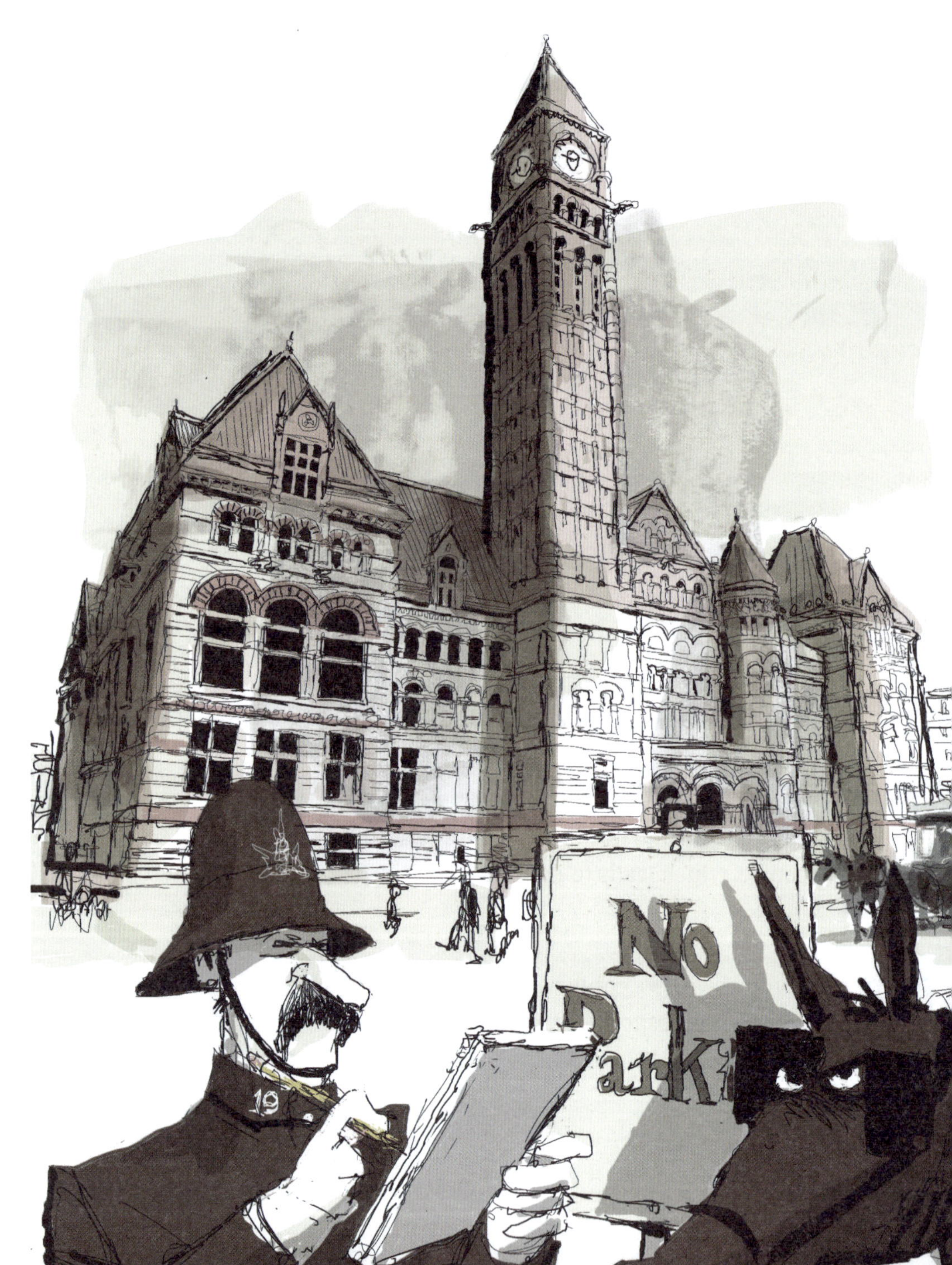

1904

THE GREAT FIRE OF TORONTO

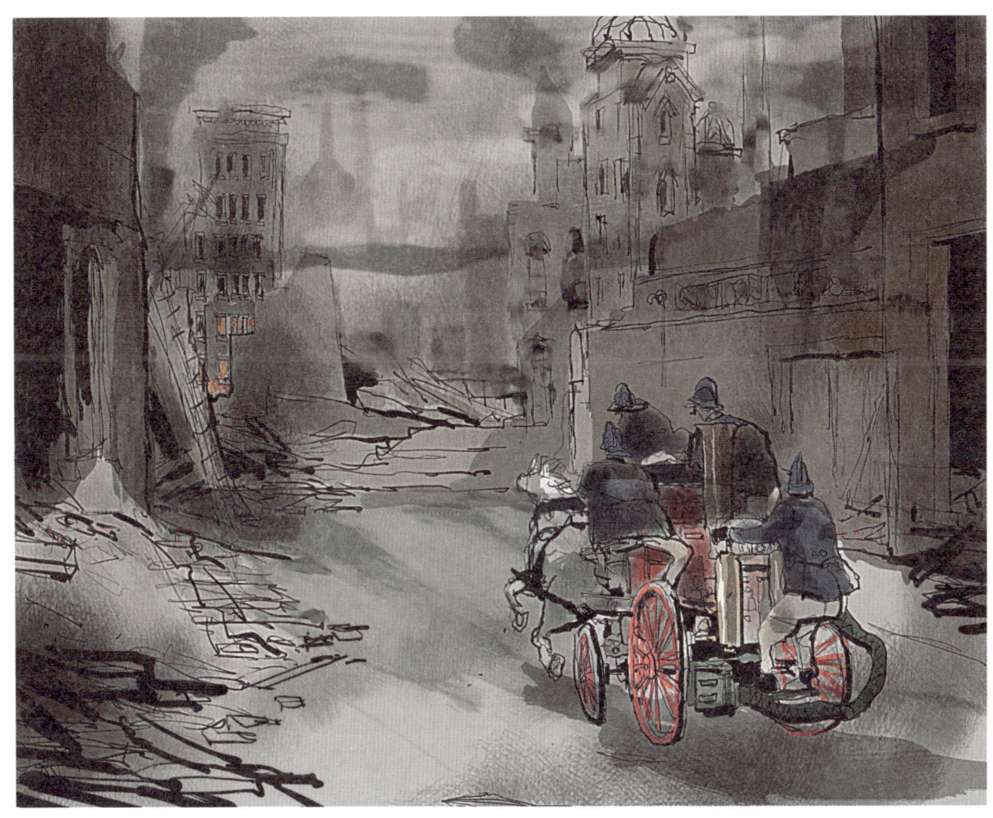

On the night of April 19, 1904, a fire starts in a building on Wellington Street in downtown Toronto. It quickly spreads to surrounding structures and before it is finally extinguished, vast numbers of businesses are destroyed and the core of the city resembles the bombed-out ruins of European cities during World War II. Astonishingly, there is no loss of life.

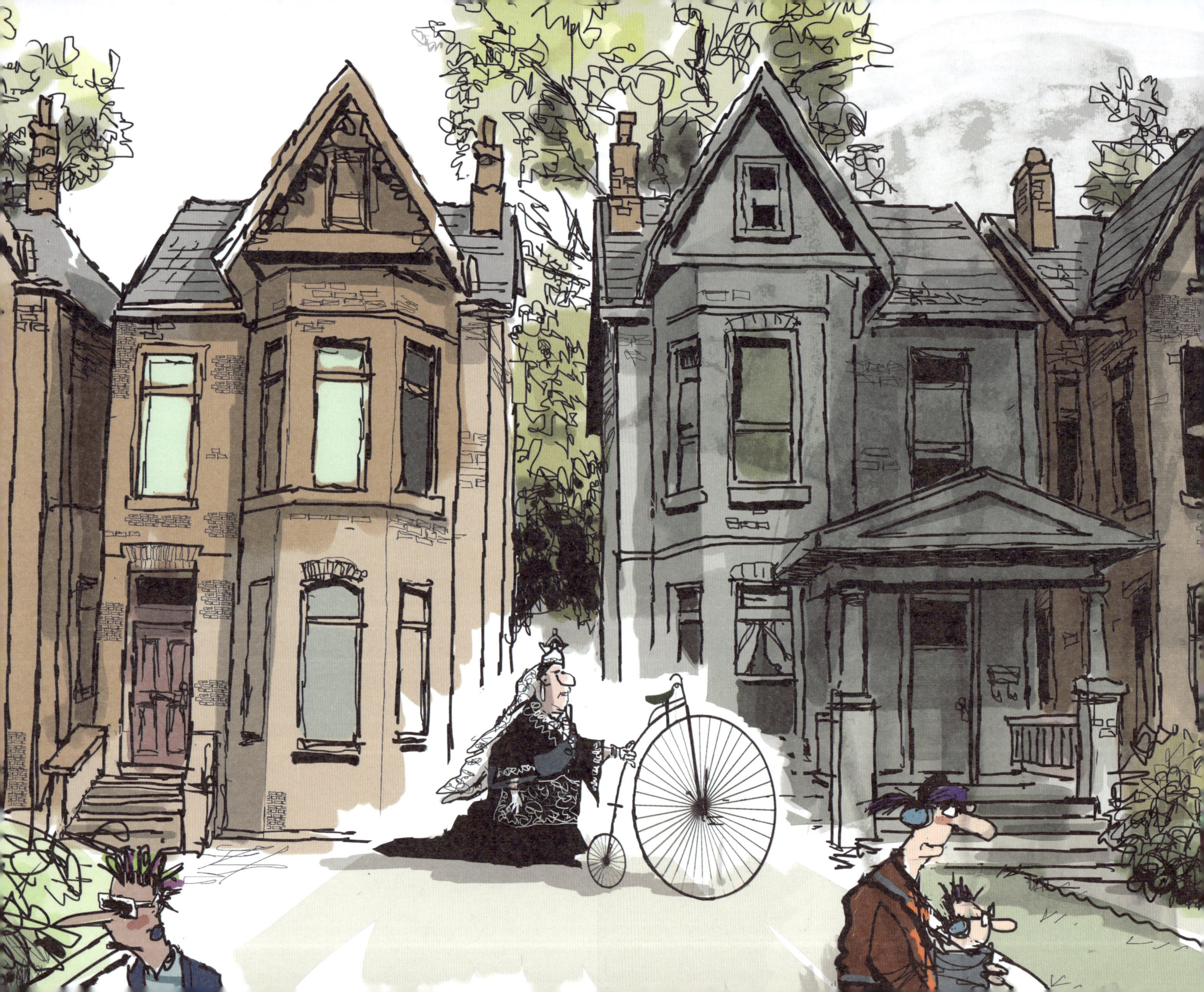

DOWNTOWN 'VICTORIANS'

After losing an estimated three quarters of the downtown in the 1904 fire, the city passes a law requiring that all newly constructed buildings must be made from bricks. Rich clay deposits in the city's Don Valley are vital in providing a source for this supply. The clay bakes into a distinct red hue, which gives a unified and unique look to the city's newly constructed streetscapes. A popular residential architectural style is based on Victorian variations and becomes known as "bay-and-gable".

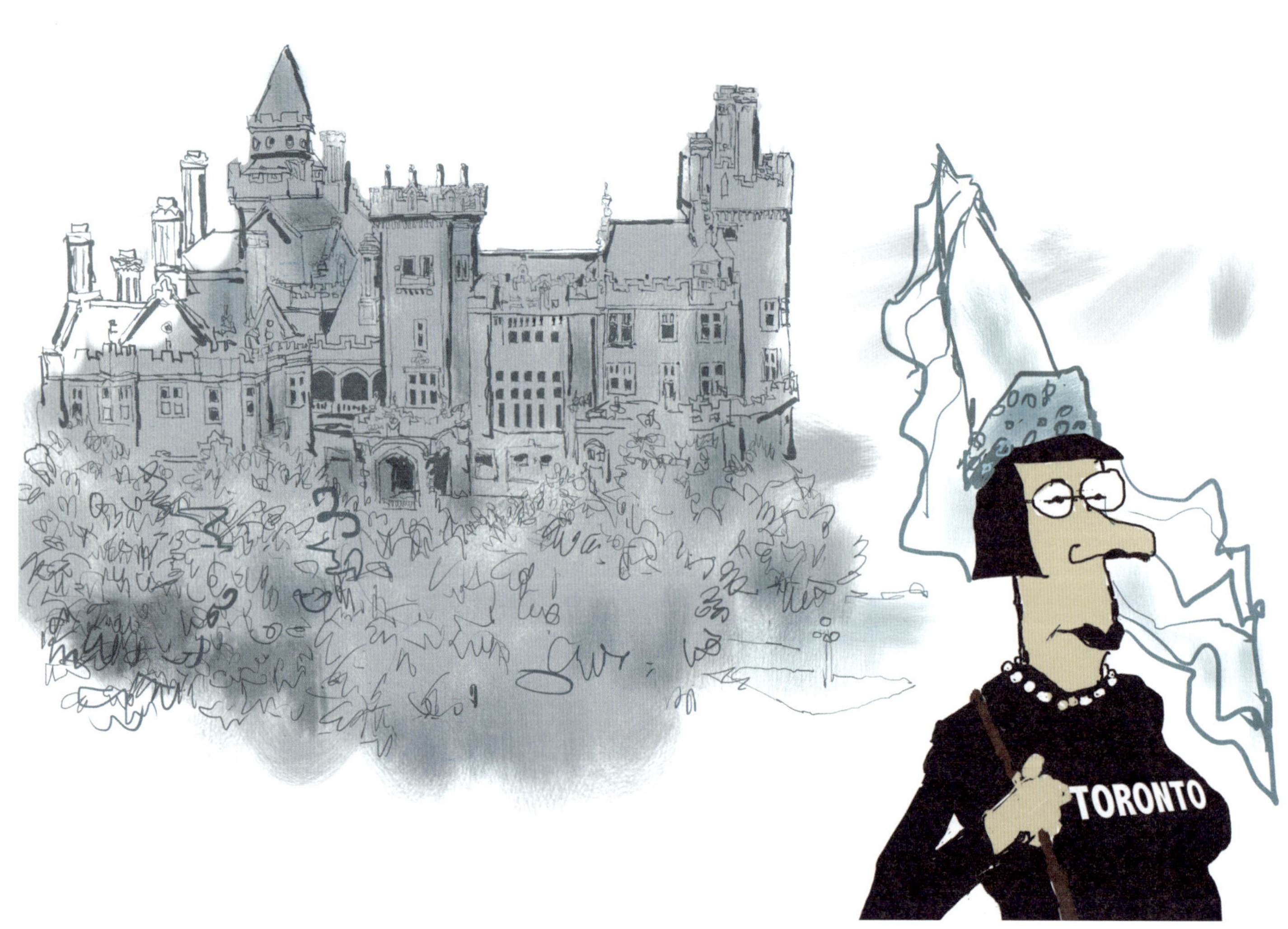
TORONTO

1914

Business man Sir Henry Pellatt builds a magnificent Gothic Revival mansion on a hill overlooking the city core. A financial depression following World War I creates difficulties in completing the project. Sir Henry is only able to live there for less than ten years, and leaves in 1923. The building goes through incarnations, briefly as a hotel and then, during prohibition, it becomes a popular nightspot for Americans.

The Toronto Islands were pivotal in Governor Simcoe's choice of a location for his defensive fort and harbour in 1793.

As the city develops the islands became a place for recreation and enjoyment. An amusement park is constructed around 1900, as well as a ten thousand-seat baseball stadium where a visiting Babe Ruth hits his first professional home run.

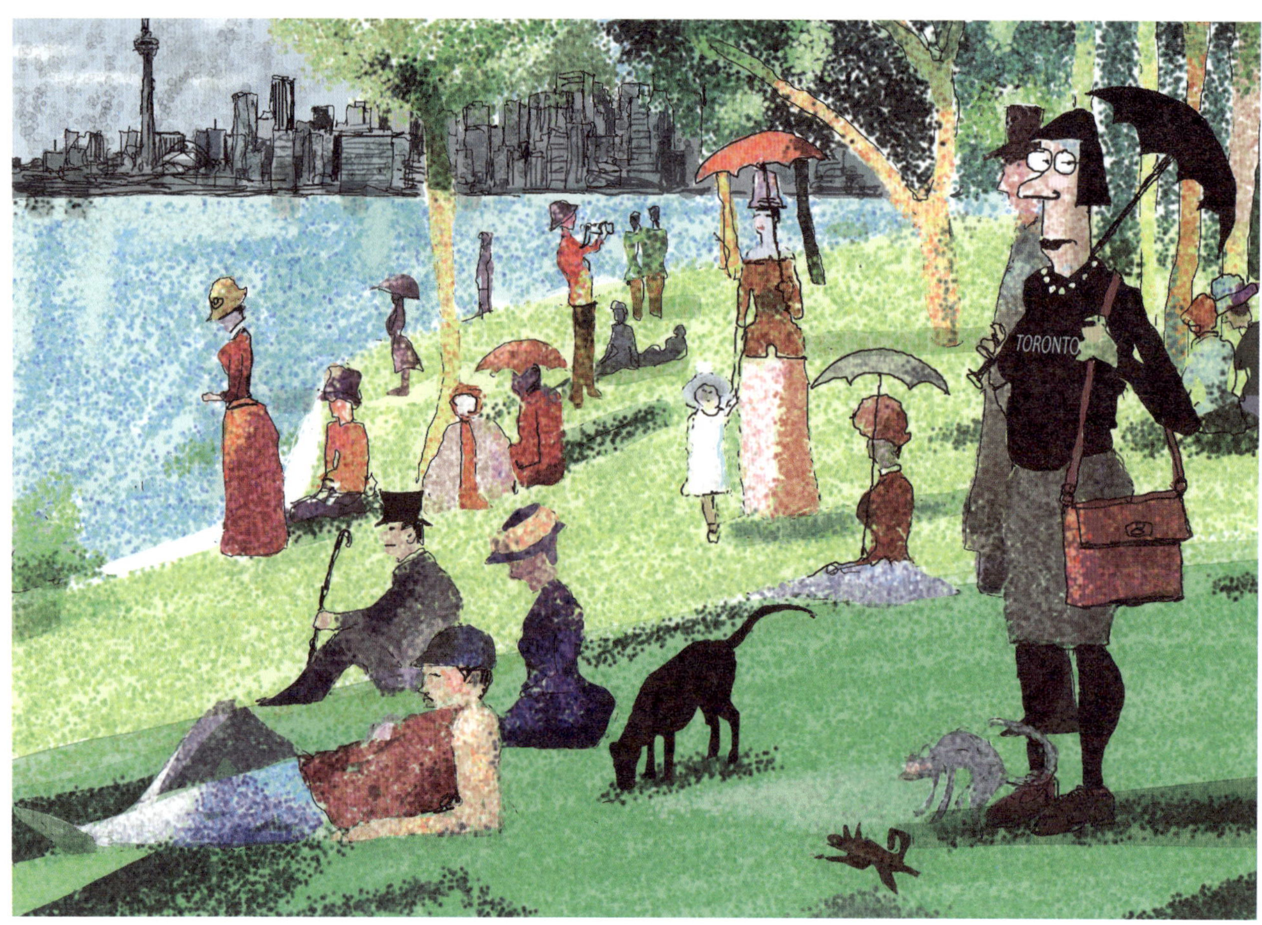

APOLOGIES TO GEORGES SEURAT

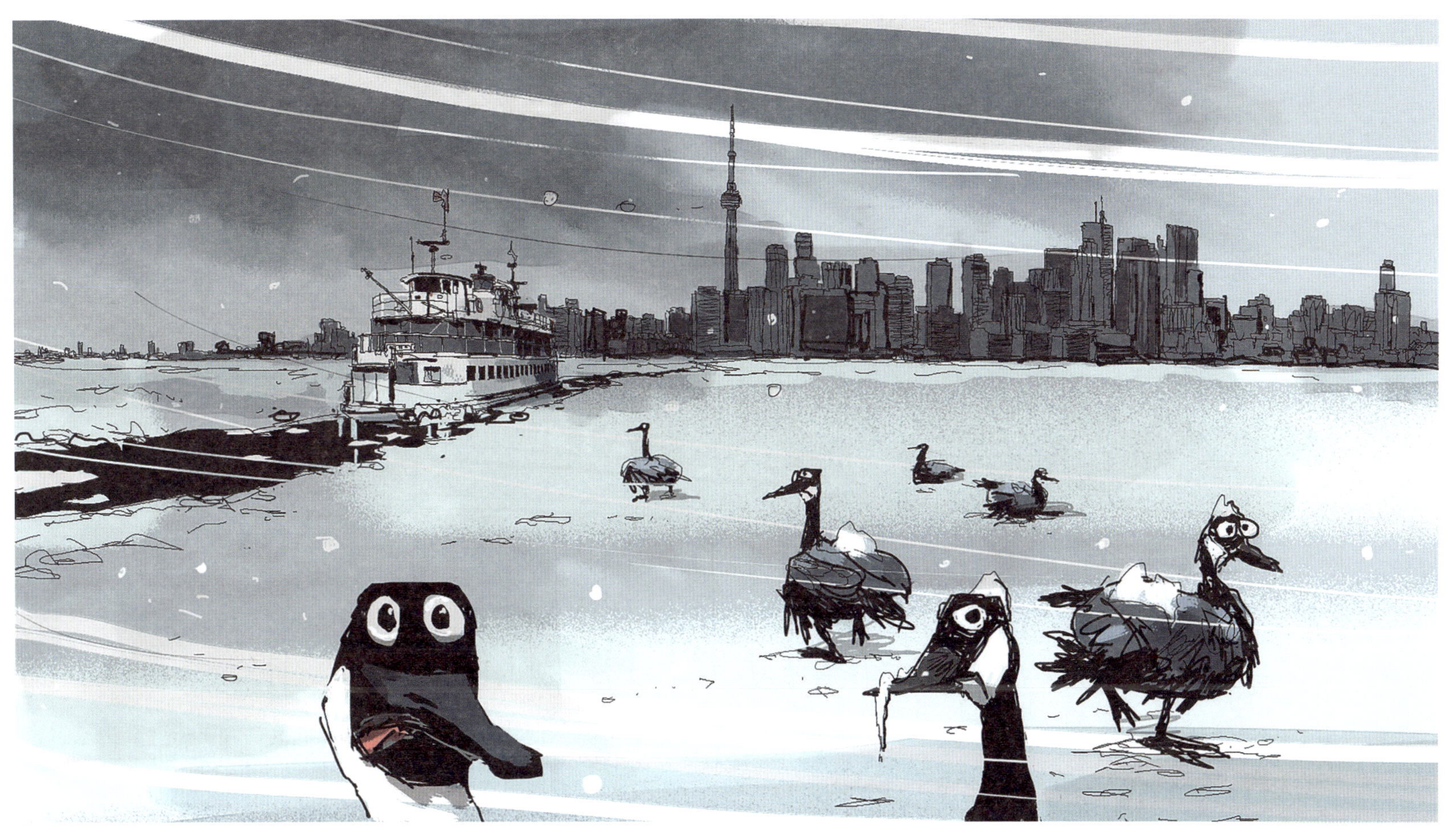

A February wind off of Lake Ontario can
make it less inviting for some.

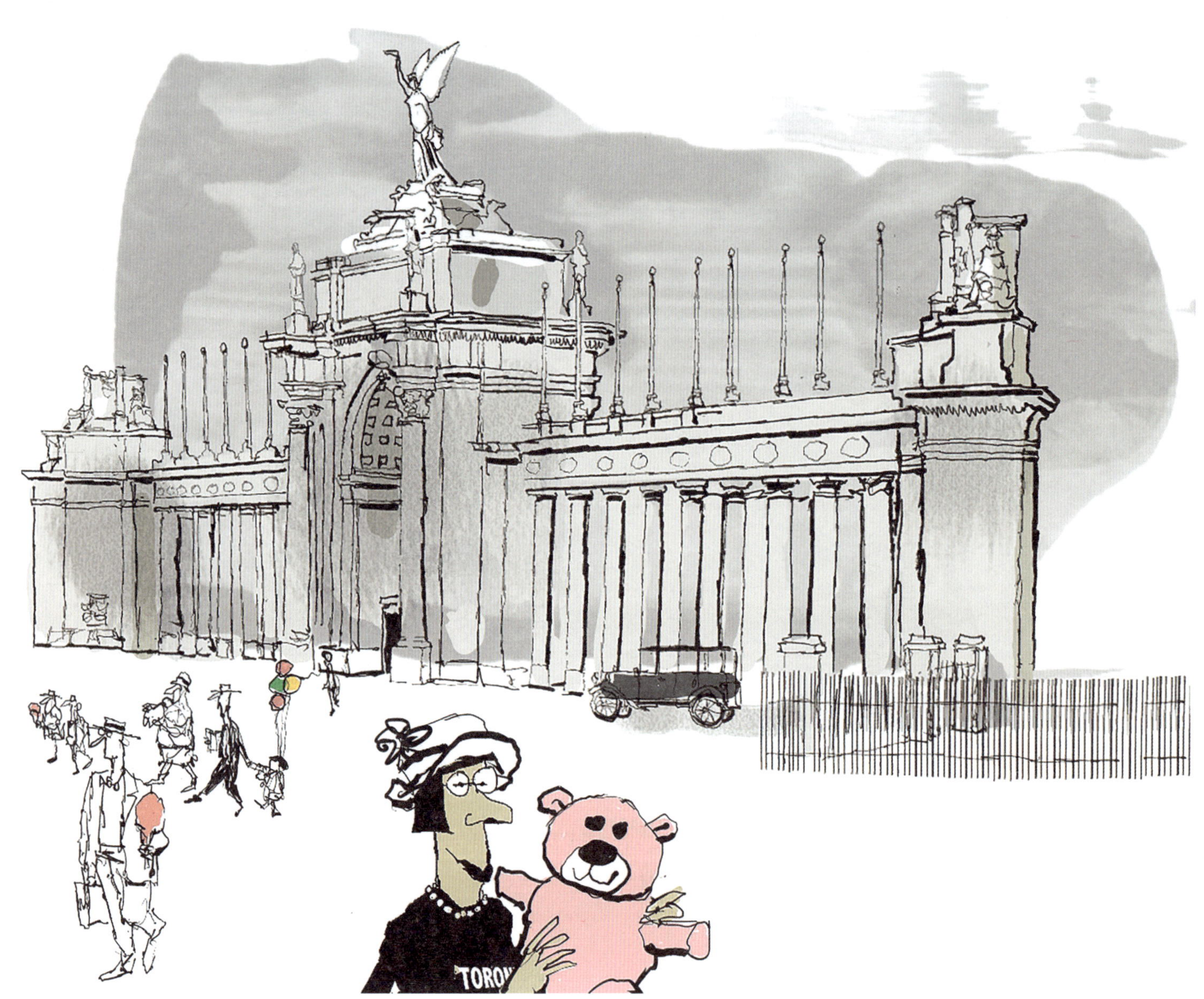
TORON

1927

THE PRINCES' GATES

The Canadian National Exhibition is established in 1879.

In 1927, the city decides to construct grand entrance gates to the fairgrounds, which are located near the Fort York site. Though many refer to the structure as the "Princess Gates," they are named in honour of Edward, Prince of Wales and Prince George, Duke of Kent. Both princes attend the official opening on August 30, 1927.

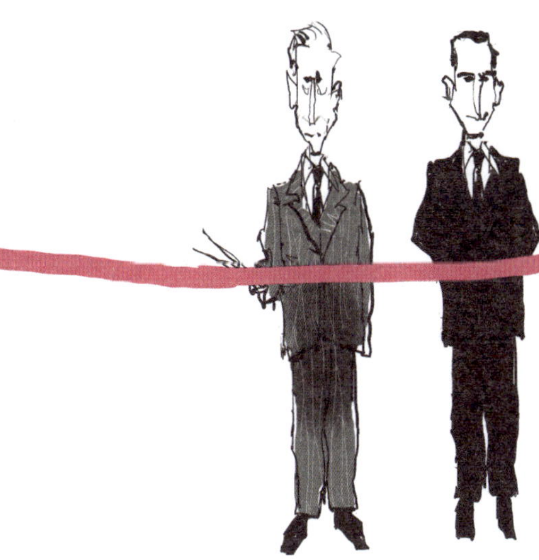

1931

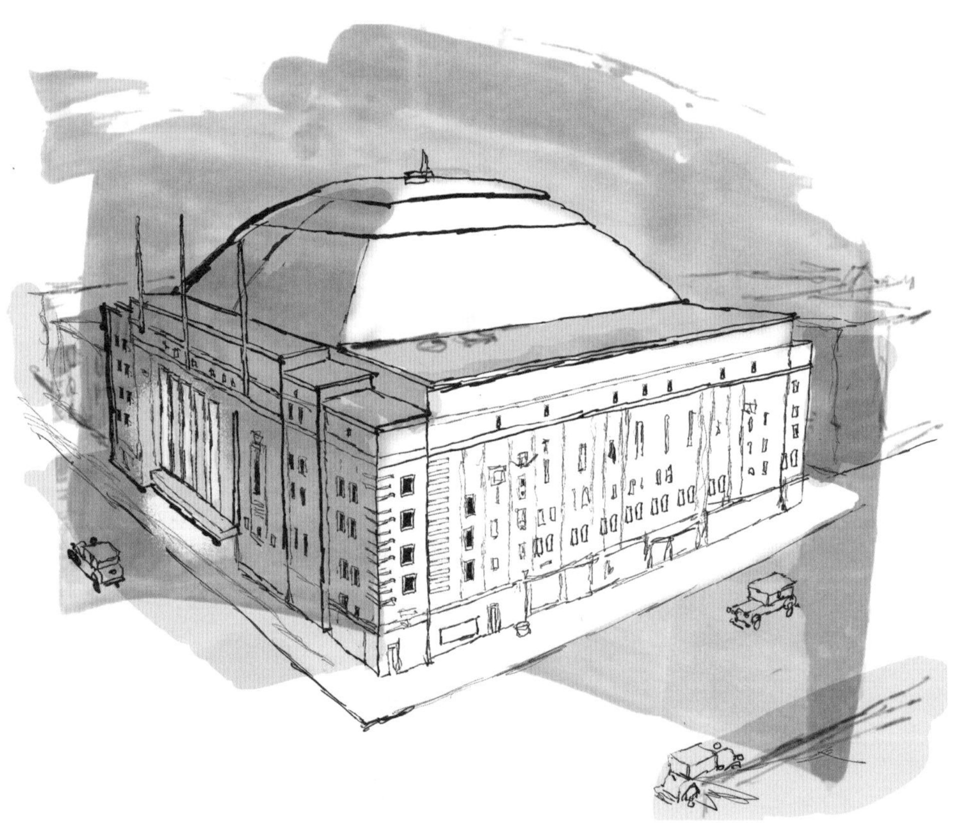

The Maple Leaf Gardens are officially opened.

Foster Hewitt becomes the voice of hockey with a career lasting forty years.

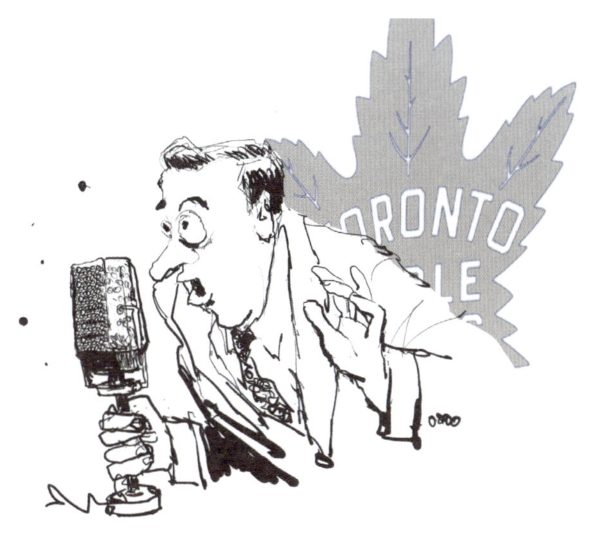

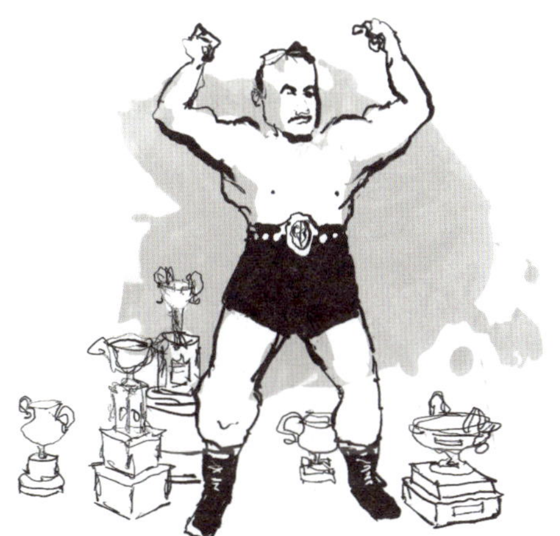

Professional wrestling draws huge crowds.

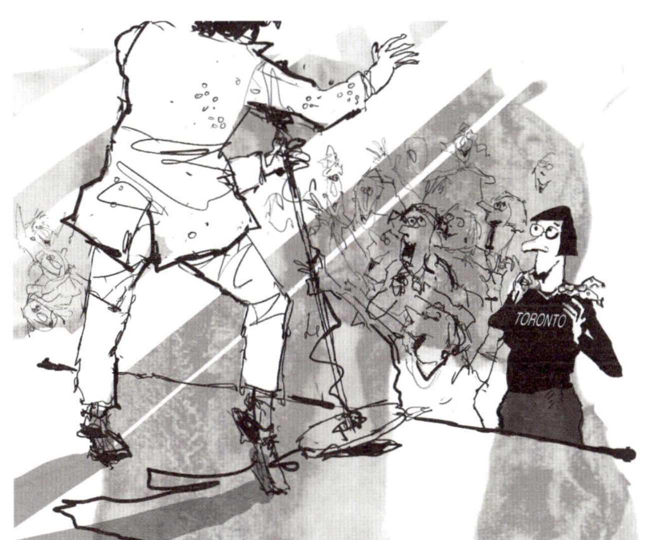

Elvis Presley rocks the Gardens in 1957.

Since their last Stanley Cup victory in 1967, Toronto hockey fans have endured an annual cycle of optimism, anxiety and, ultimately, despair. Each NHL season has seen precisely the same distressing pattern.

I drew the cartoon below for the *Globe and Mail* during Easter in 2014 as the Leaf's playoff juggernaut began to lose momentum.

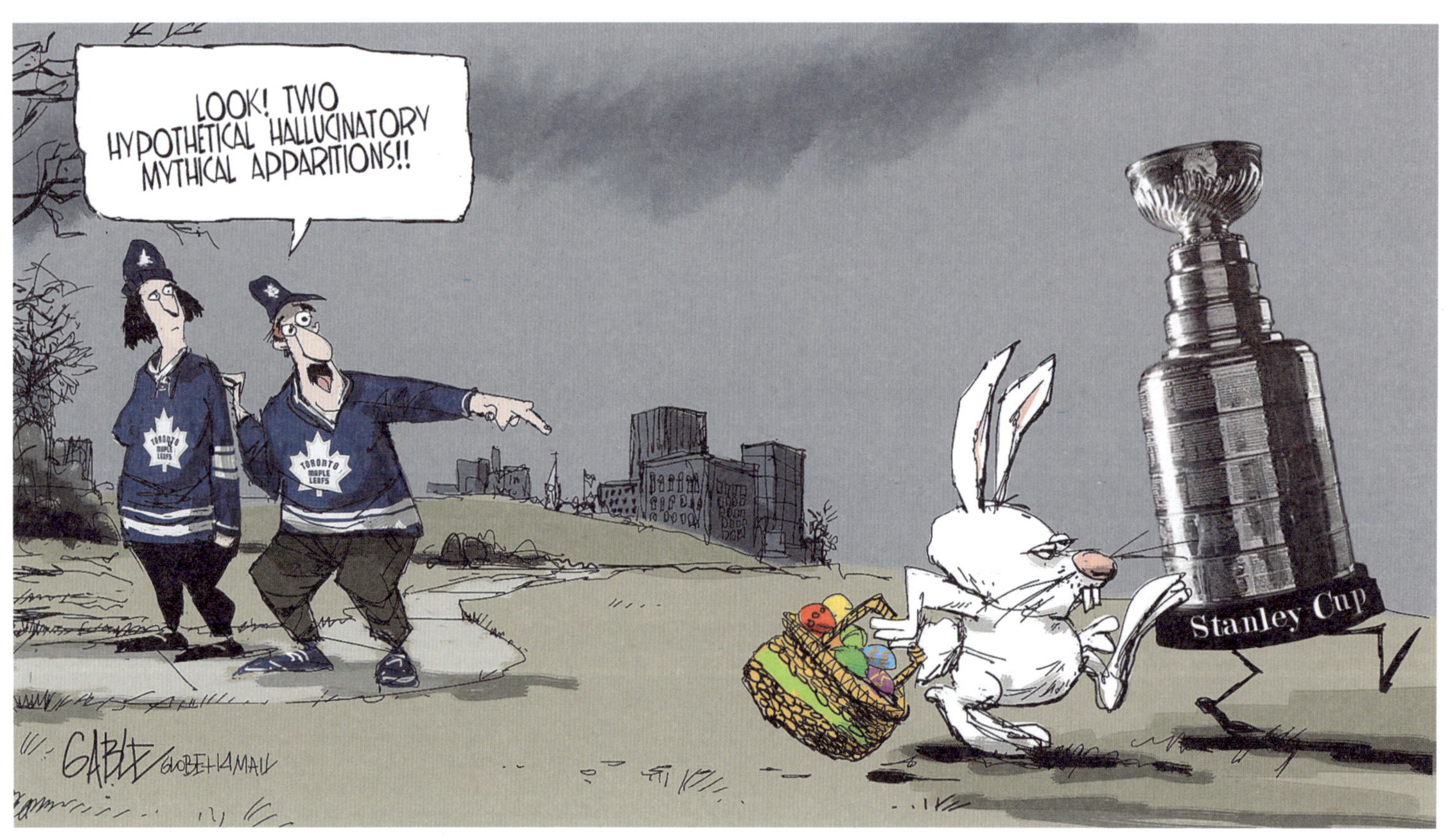

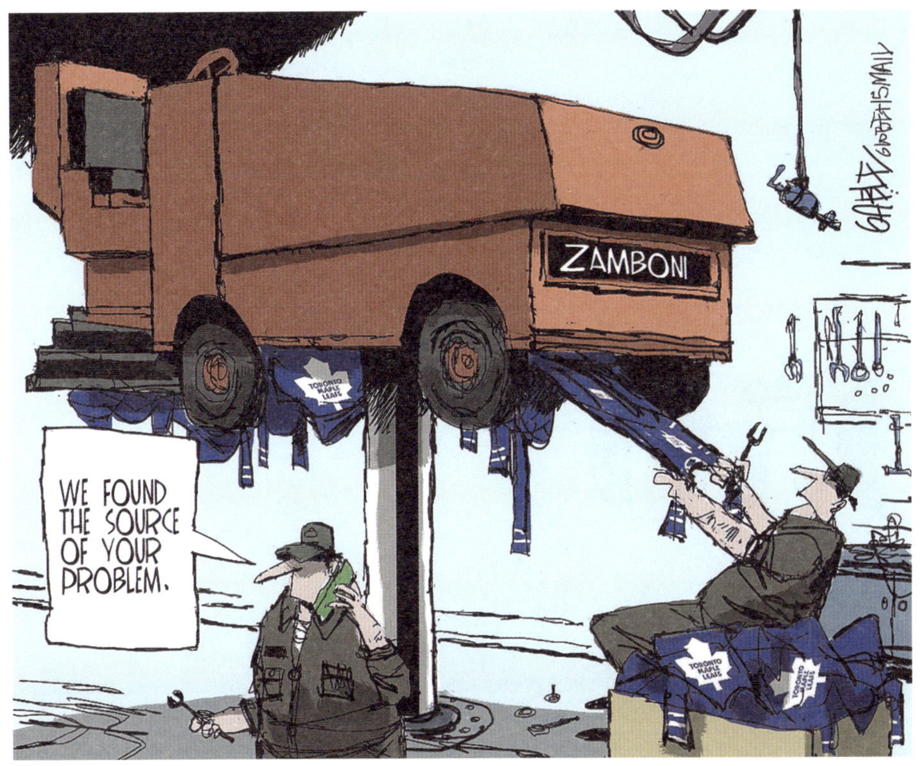

As a symbol of their frustration during lacklustre games, some fans took to hurling their Leafs jerseys onto the ice.

MONTREAL TAXI DRIVER: "WHERE ARE YOU FROM?"

PASSENGER: "TORONTO."

DRIVER: "WHERE'S THE RED LIGHT DISTRICT IN TORONTO?"

PASSENGER: "NOT SURE."

DRIVER: "BEHIND THE LEAFS GOAL NET."

1950

Following the end of World War ll, Toronto receives increasing waves of immigration from abroad.

These new arrivals introduce aspects of their cultures into the urban life of the city.

The first patio cafe.

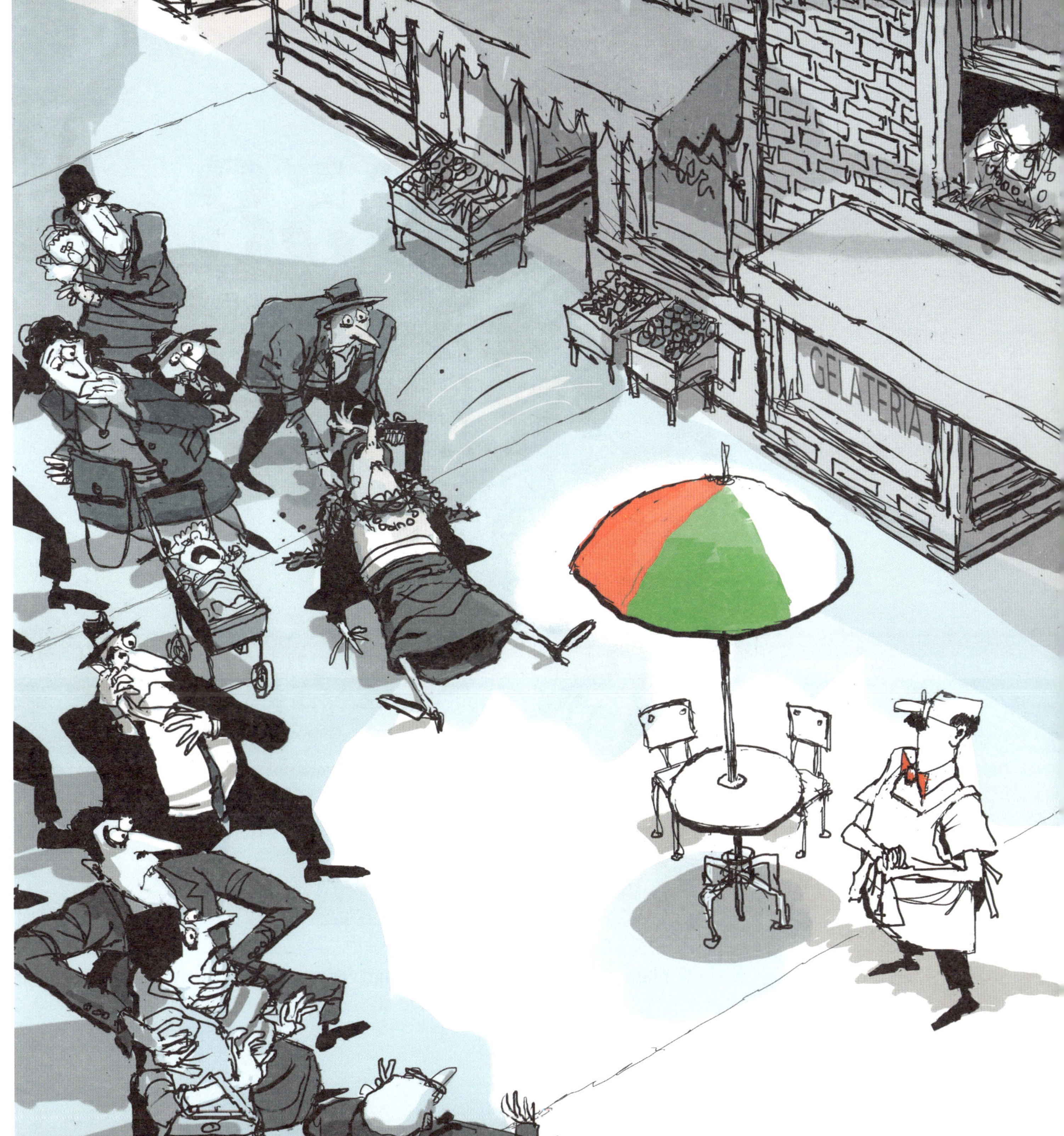

1958

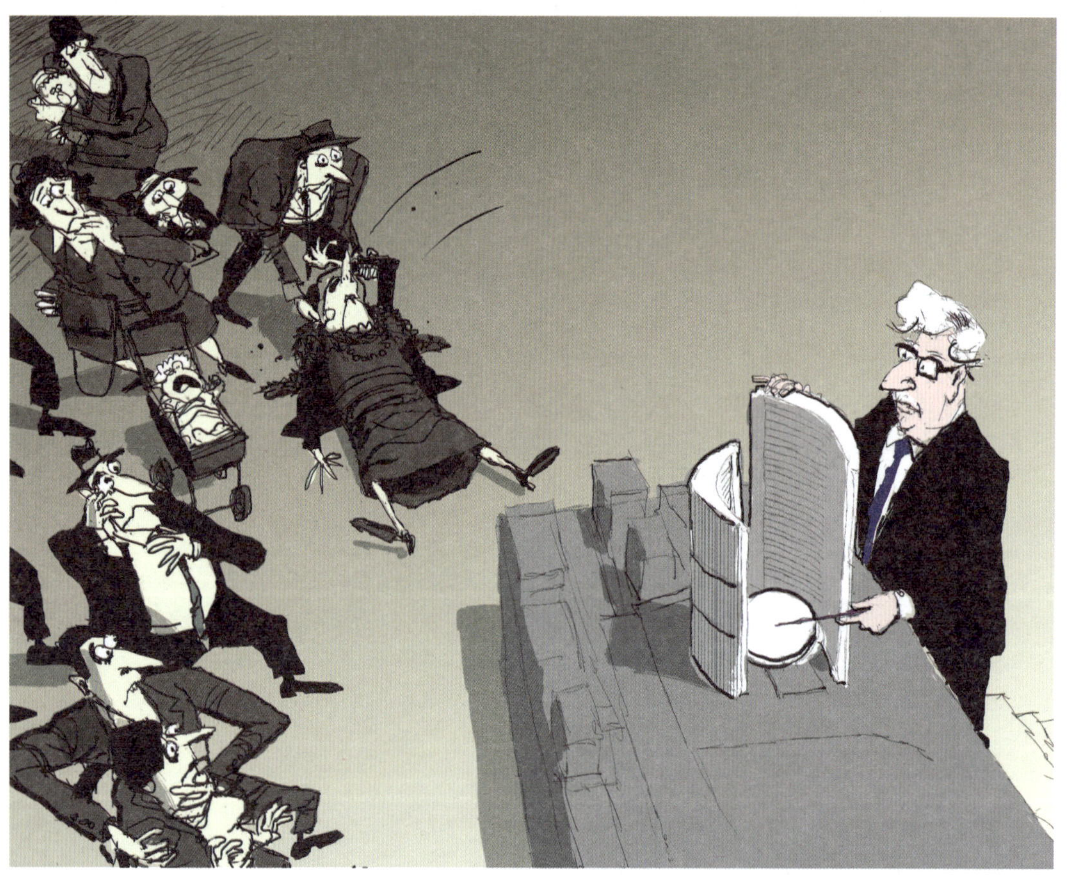

Finland's Viljo Revell wins the design competition for Toronto's new City Hall.

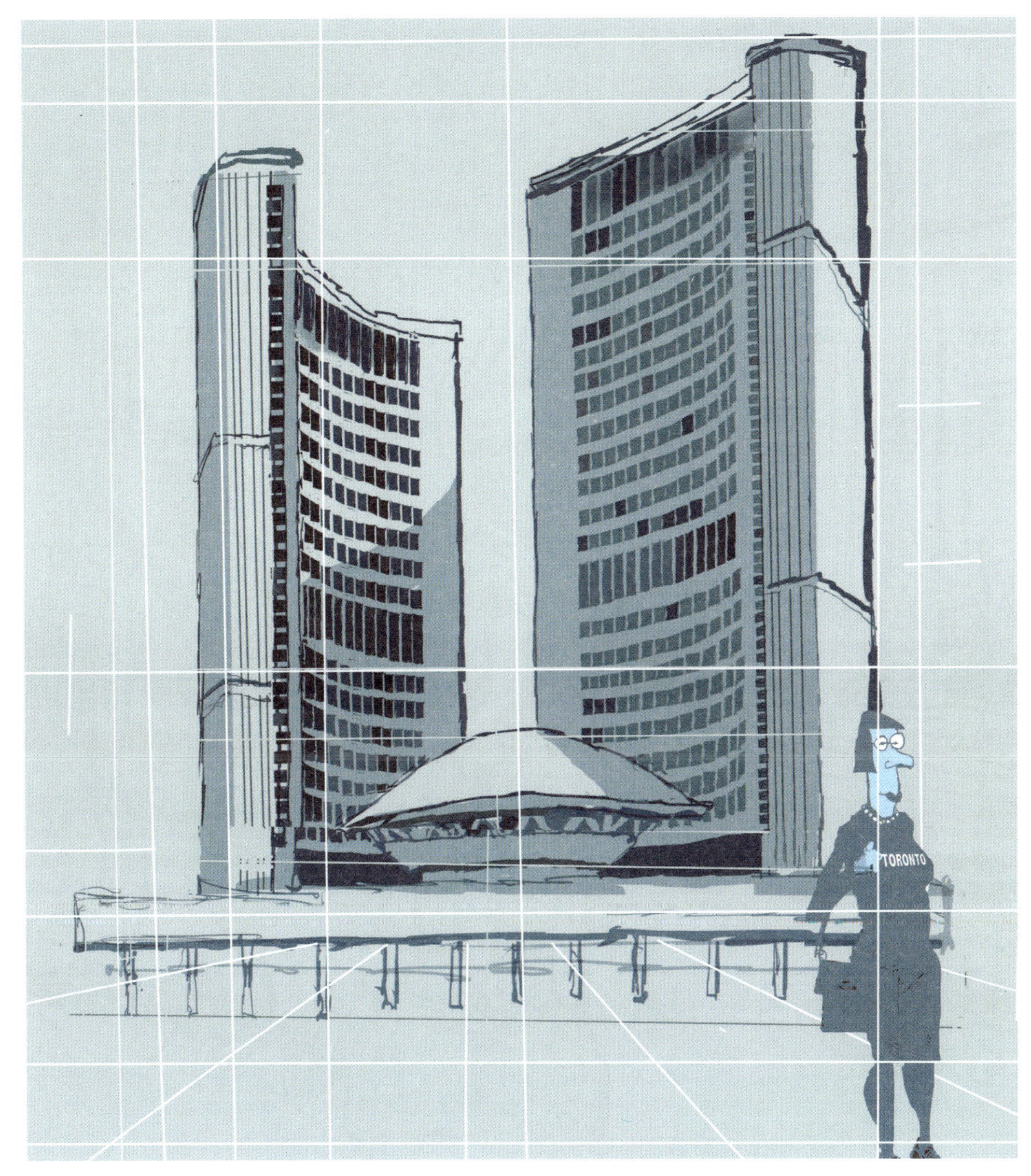
TORONTO

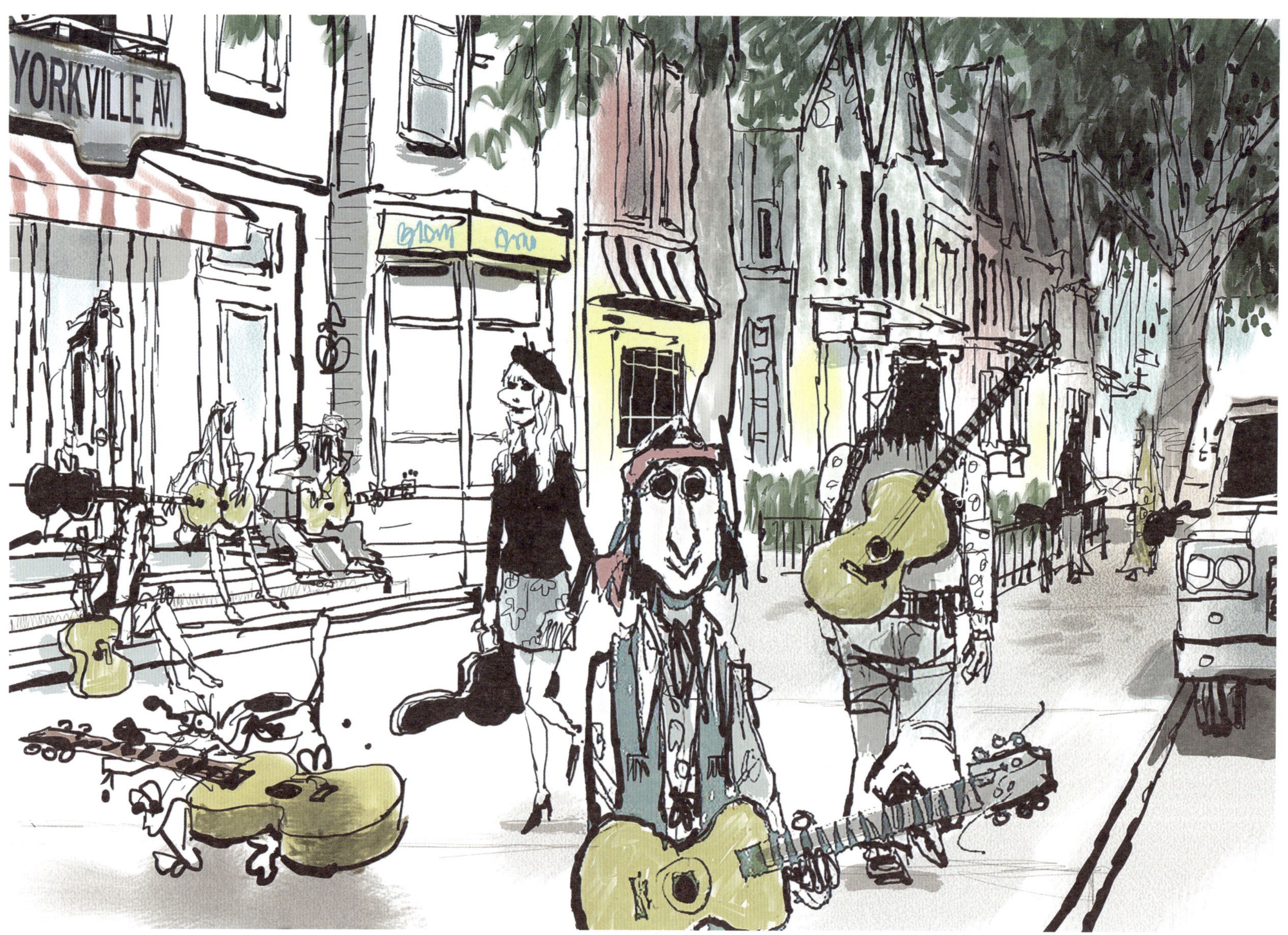
YORKVILLE AV.

1960

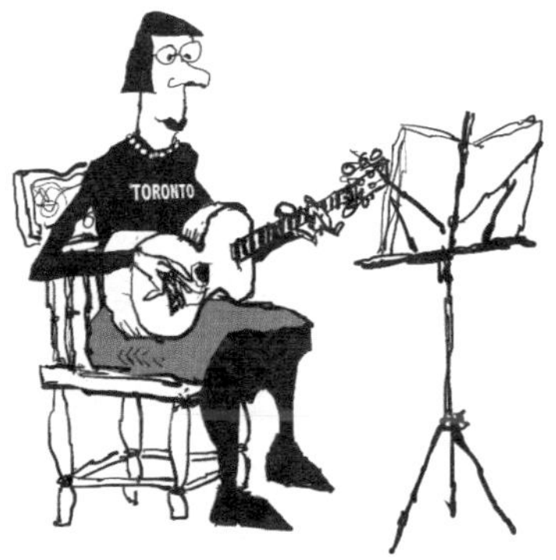

Folk music, rock, the British Invasion and pop culture . . .
life begins to speed up in the city.

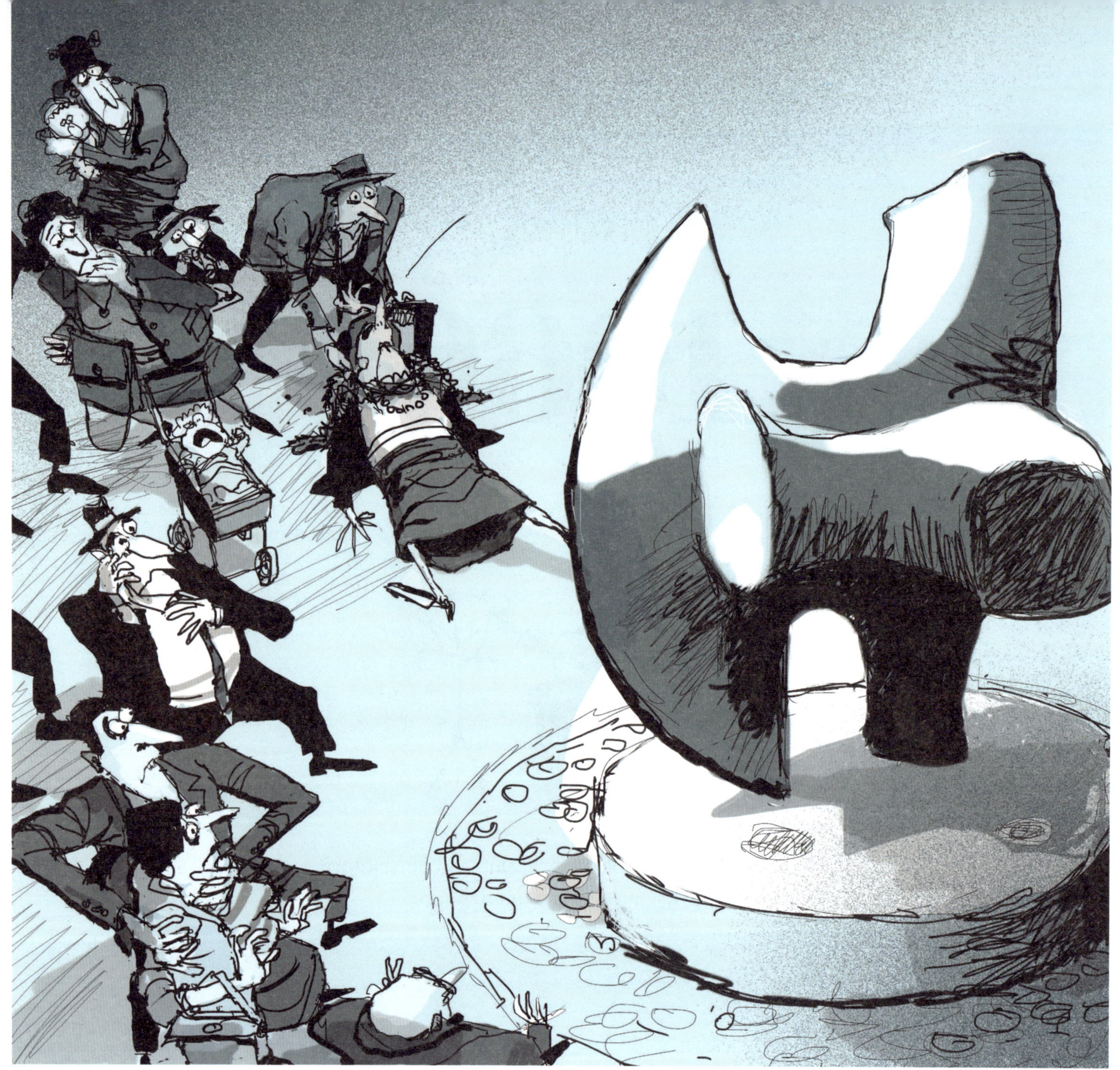

1964

Henry Moore's "The Archer" is selected to adorn Nathan Philips Square in front of the newly opened city hall. The sculpture is regarded as too radical by some elements of the citizenry.

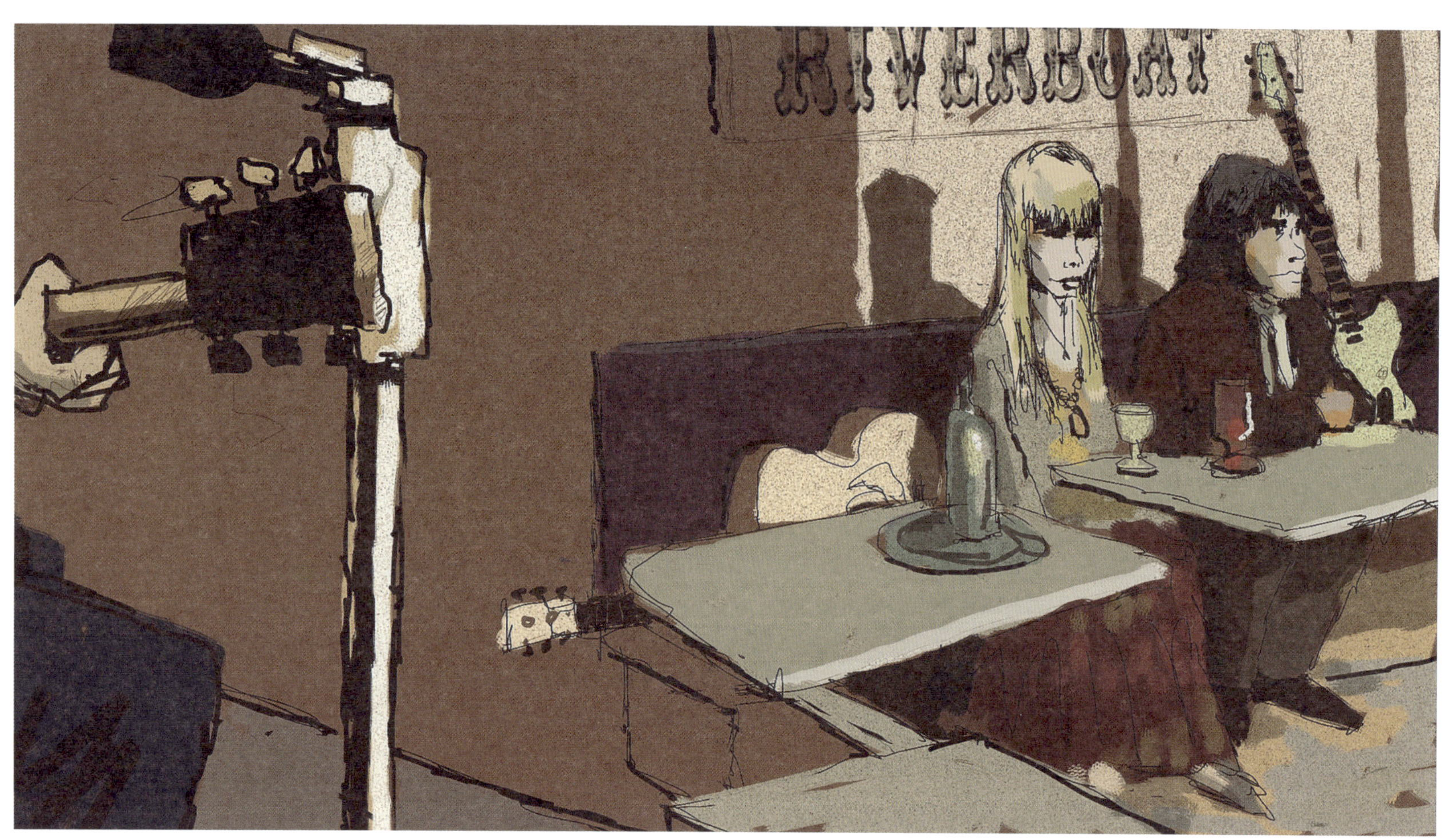
RIVERBOAT

1966

Along with art galleries and fashion boutiques, Yorkville is home to a number of music venues and coffee houses which launch the international careers of a number of musicians. The Purple Onion, The Penny Farthing, and The Riverboat become creative hubs which stage innumerable performances from rising stars, both local and from abroad.

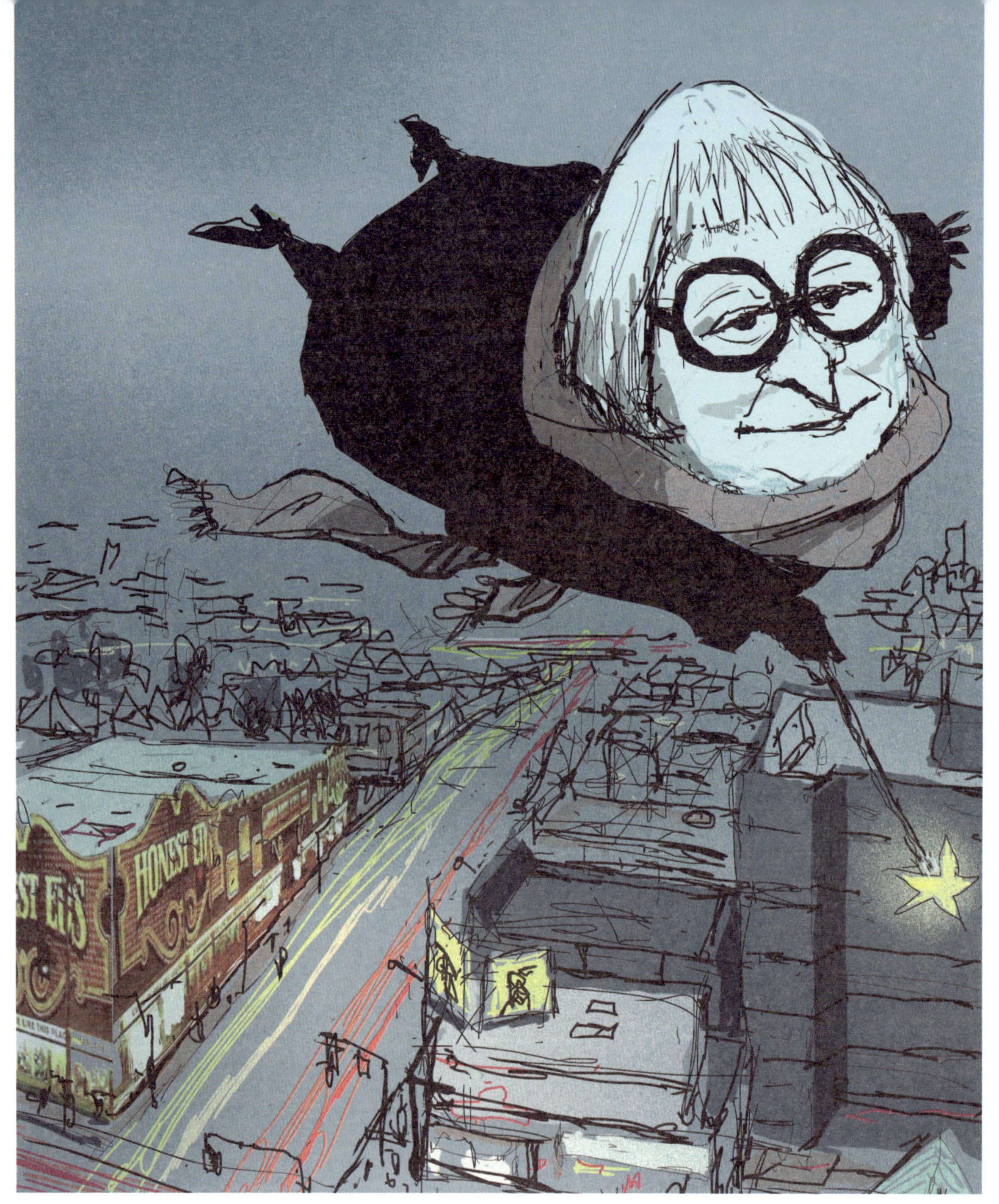
EST ED'S
HONEST ED
E LIKE THIS PLAC

1969

Jane Jacobs, author of *The Death and Life of Great American Cities*, moves to Toronto from New York City. She becomes a central figure in preserving a vast area of the city's core from the proposed Spadina expressway expansion. Her writing and lectures inspire a generation of citizens to appreciate the importance of making urban spaces inviting and exciting environments to live in.

Just west of the downtown core is the Kensington Market neighbourhood. This area has a long history of welcoming successive waves of immigrants, as well as embodying a bohemian lifestyle.

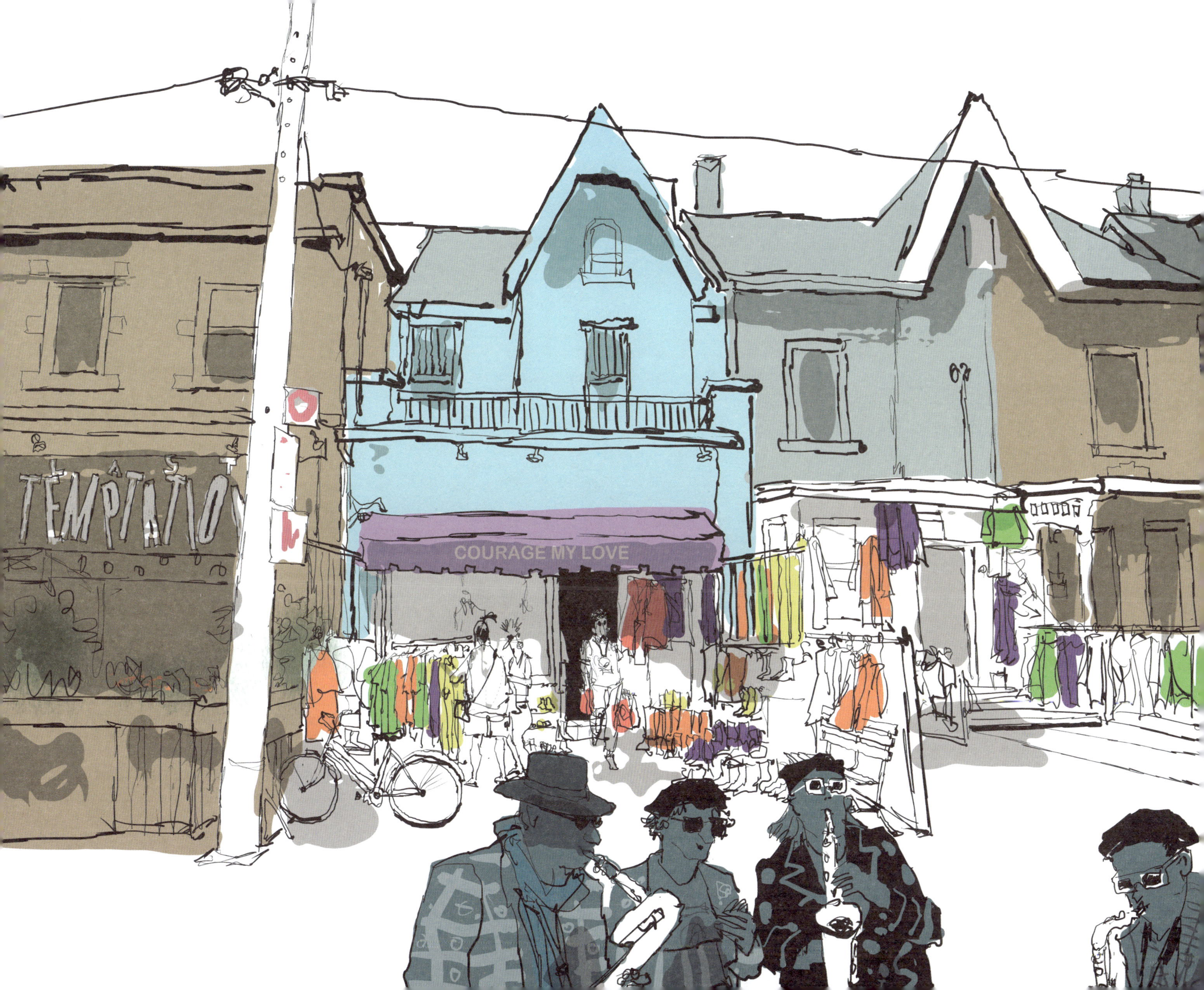
COURAGE MY LOVE

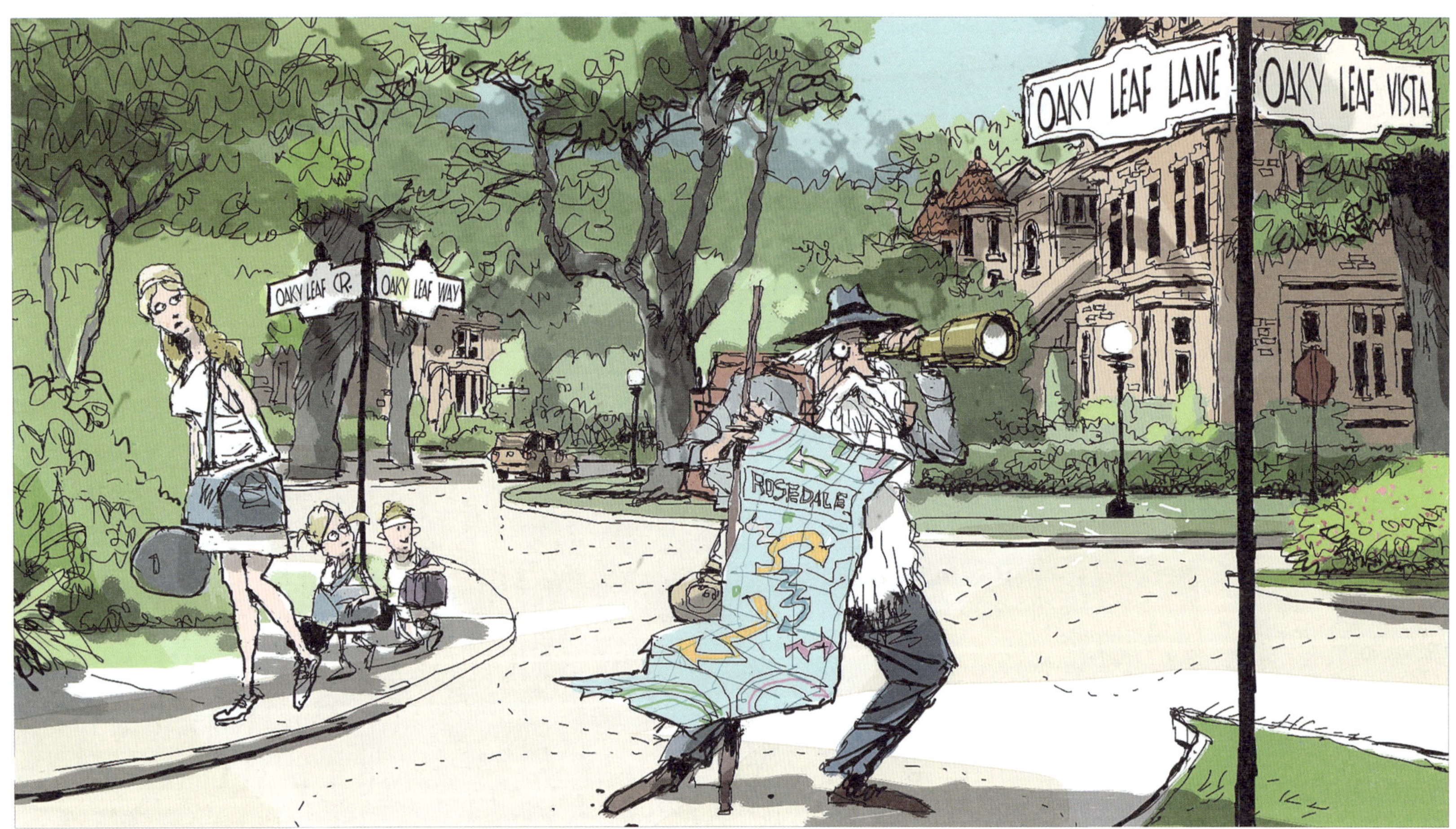

Most of Toronto conforms to its initial grid layout. The most well known exception is the neighbourhood of Rosedale where the winding streets can be confusing for the uninitiated.

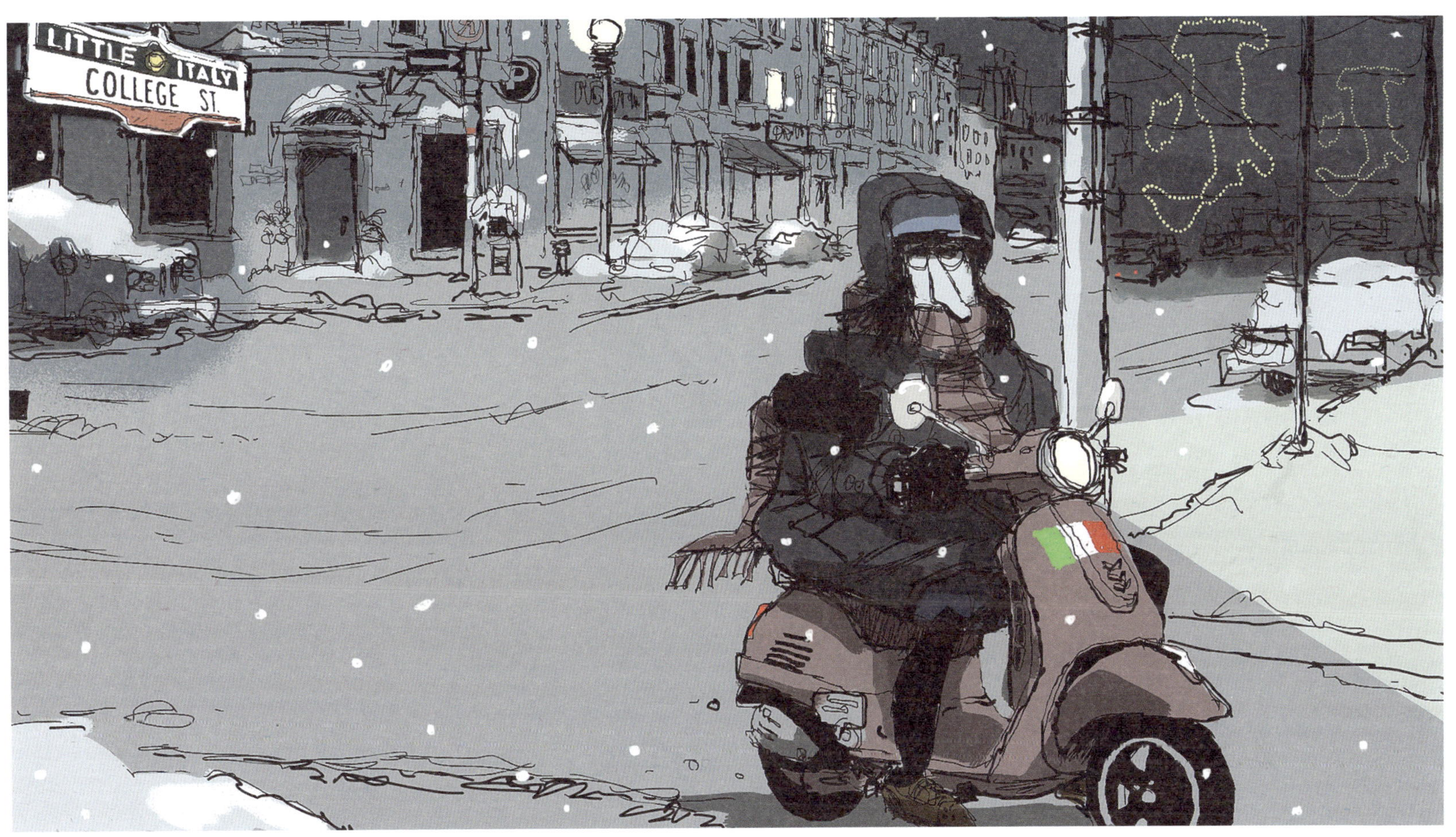

While some areas of the city begin to reflect a more cosmopolitan style, the Canadian climate remains a constraining factor.

1970

Yonge Street, the city's main thoroughfare, is filled with record stores and music venues and comes to life at night.

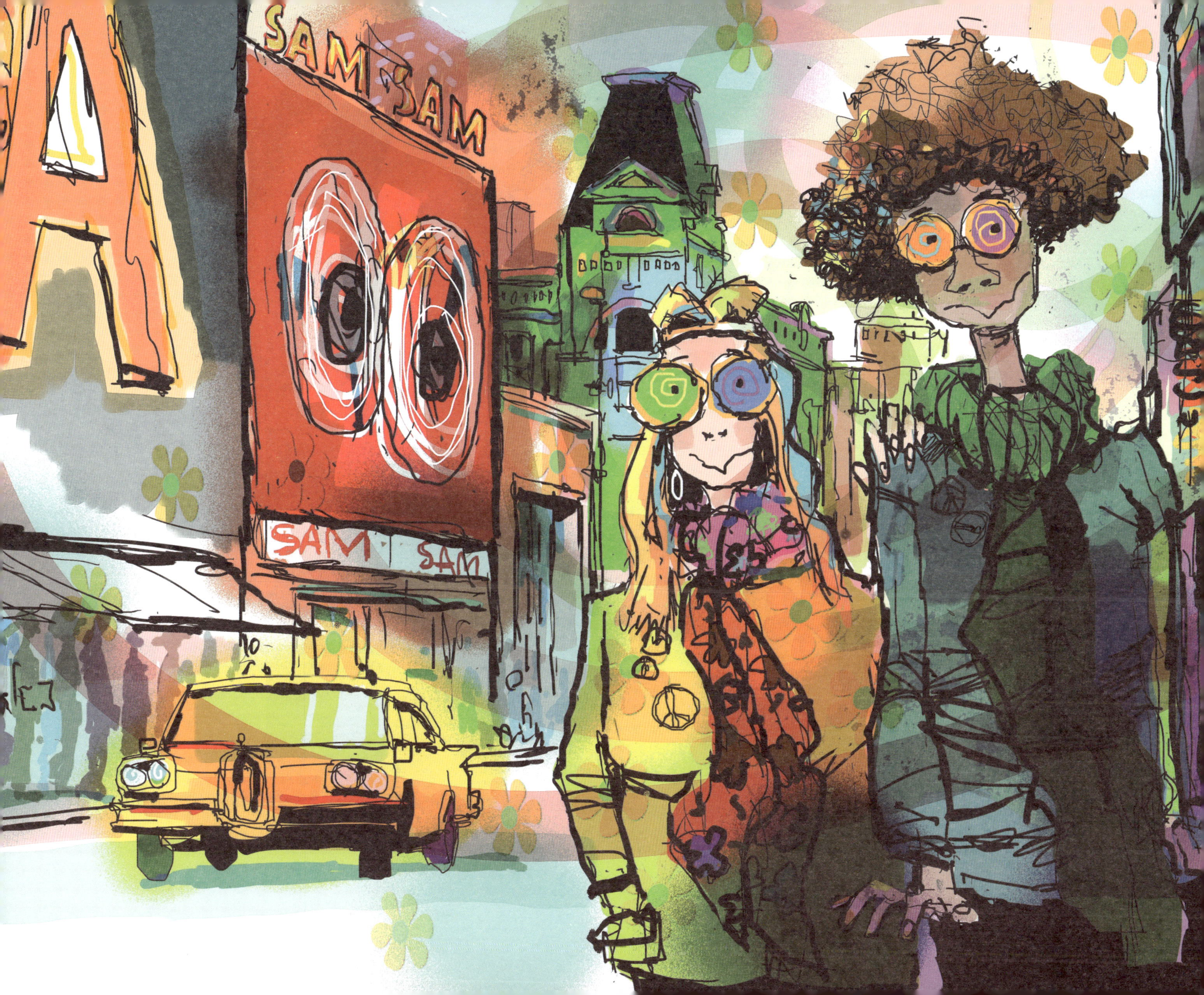
SAM SAM
SAM
SAM

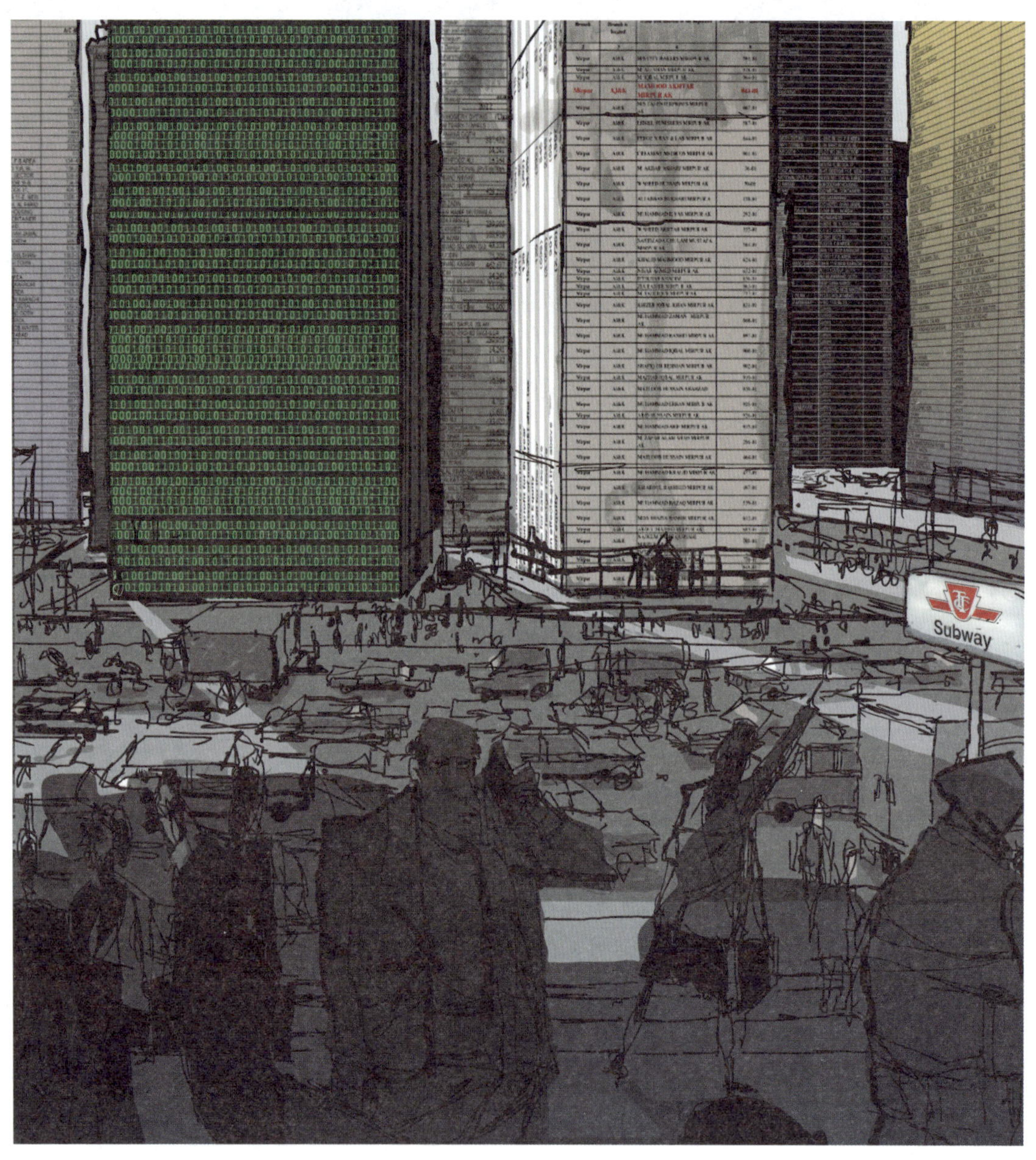
Subway

1976

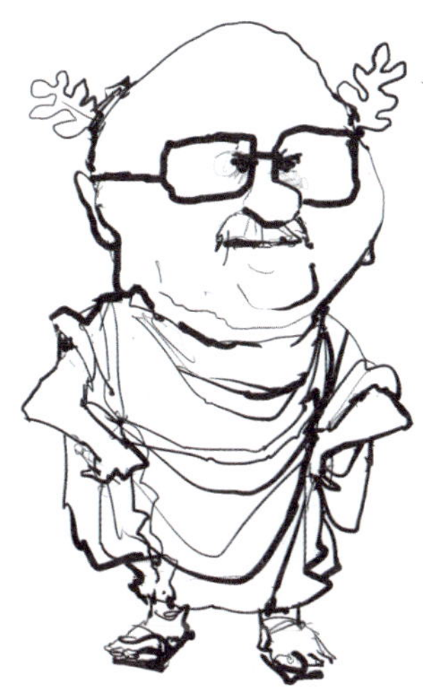

DURING THE LATE NINETEEN SEVENTIES MONTREAL BEGINS TO LOSE INCREASING NUMBERS OF CORPORATE HEAD OFFICES TO TORONTO AS QUEBEC'S LANGUAGE POLICIES INTENSIFY. MAYOR JEAN DRAPEAU'S RESPONSE AT THE TIME IS:

"LET TORONTO BECOME MILAN. MONTREAL WILL ALWAYS BE ROME."

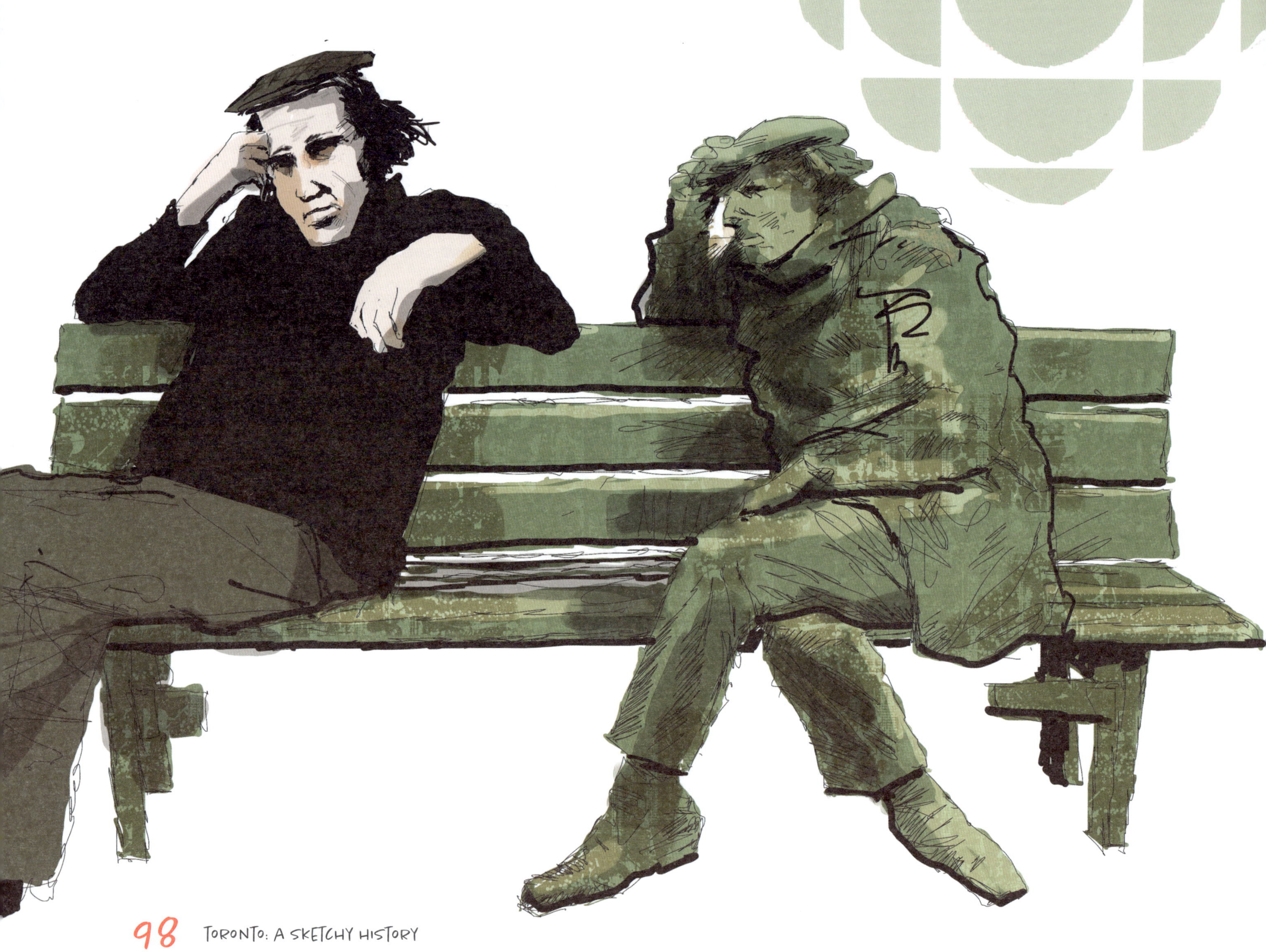

1977

Toronto pianist, Glenn Gould, achieves international and stellar recognition when his recording of Bach's *The Well-Tempered Clavier* is launched into the universe aboard NASA's space probe "Voyager."

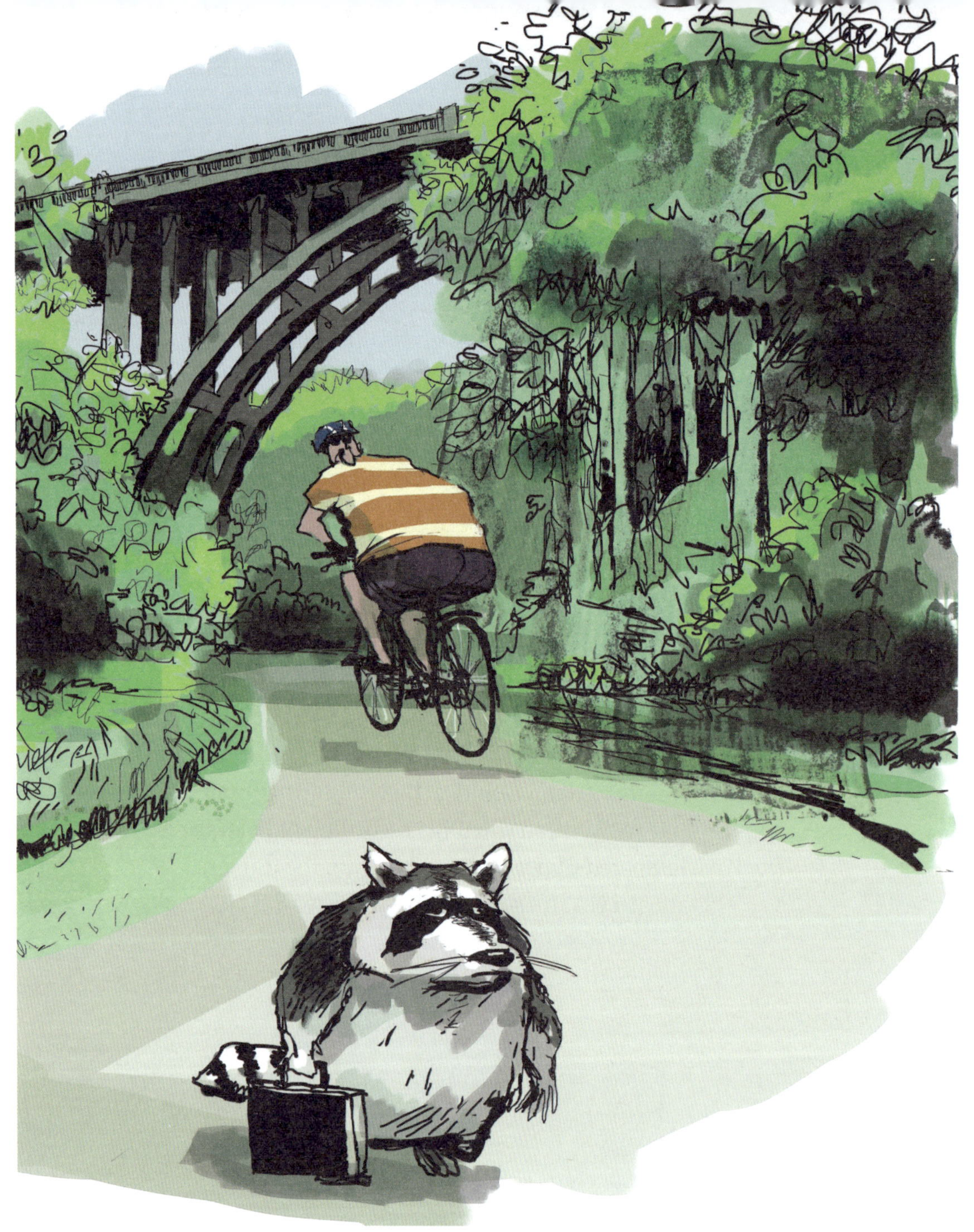

The city's vast and often overlooked ravine system is home to an array of thriving natural animal species. Many of these have done a remarkable job of adapting to urban life.

1976

The CN Tower is completed.

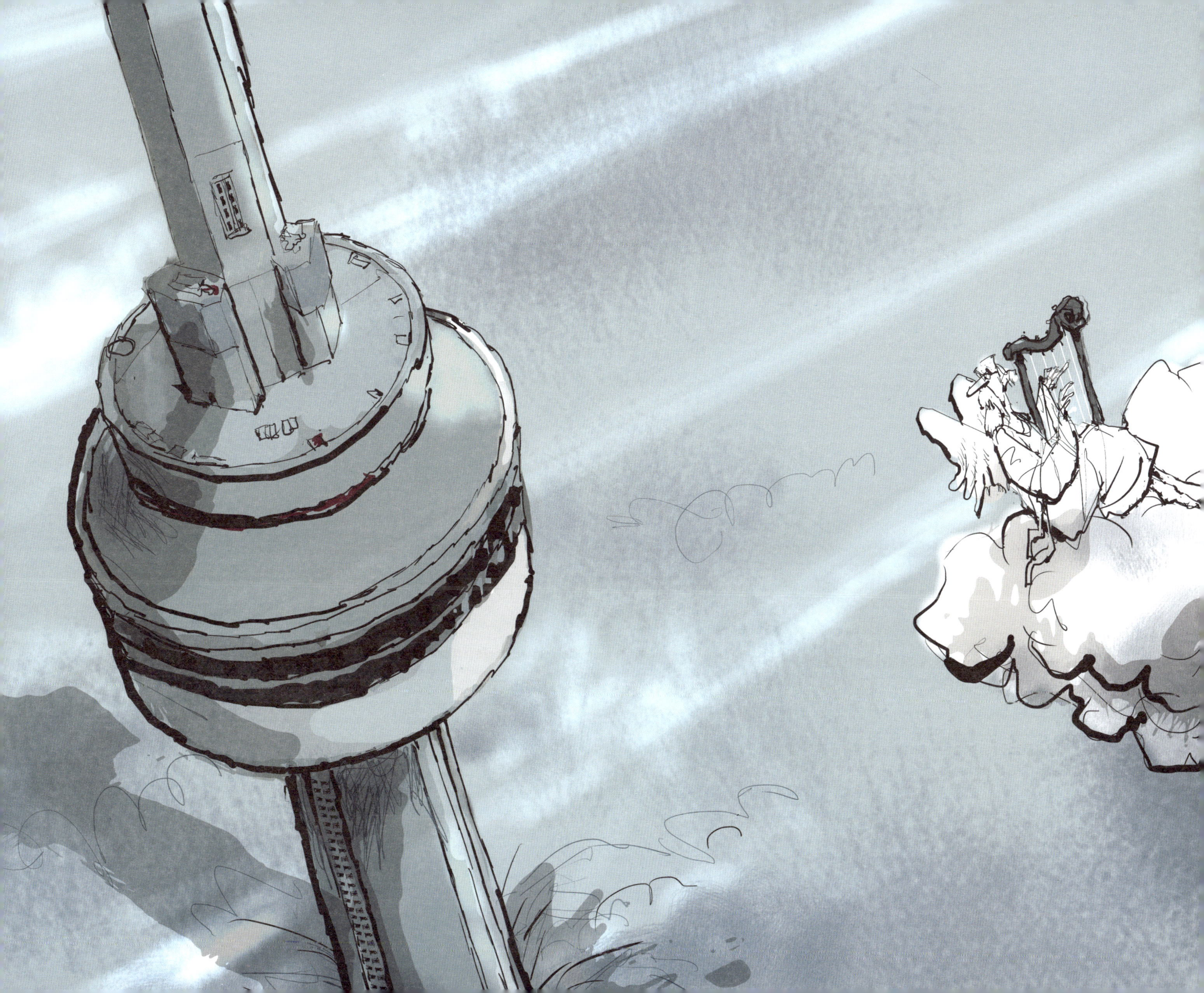

1980

Sensing its newfound potential on the international stage, Toronto increasingly gains a sense of confidence and destiny. The rest of the country responds in the usual manner.

ERIC NICOL, CANADIAN HUMOURIST AND WRITER:

"CLEARLY, IF CONFEDERATION IS TO SURVIVE ANOTHER 100 YEARS, CANADA MUST FIND A NATIONAL ESPRIT DE CORPS. COHESION CANNOT DEPEND INDEFINITELY ON HATING TORONTO."

—100 YEARS OF WHAT?, 1966

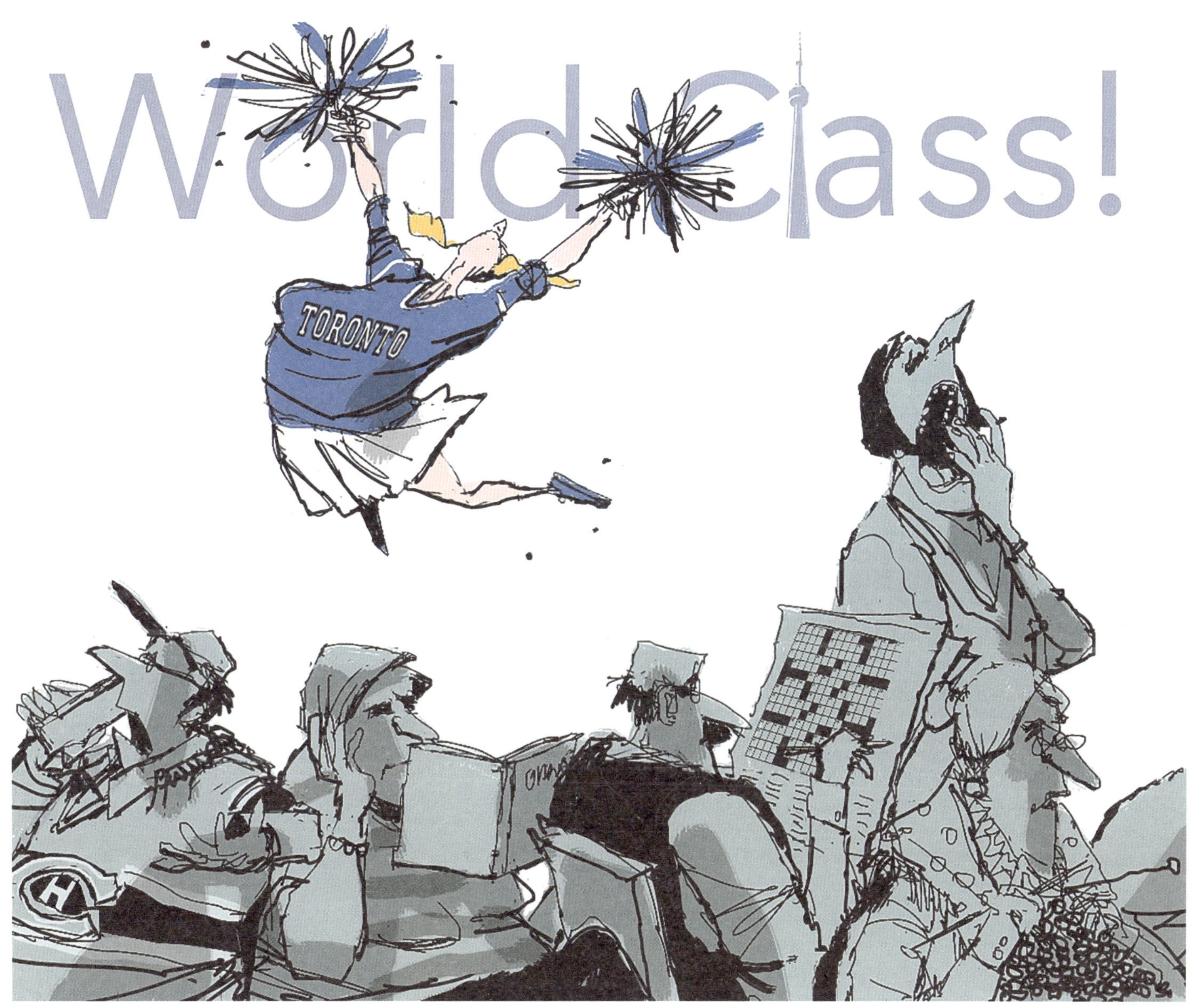
World Class!
TORONTO

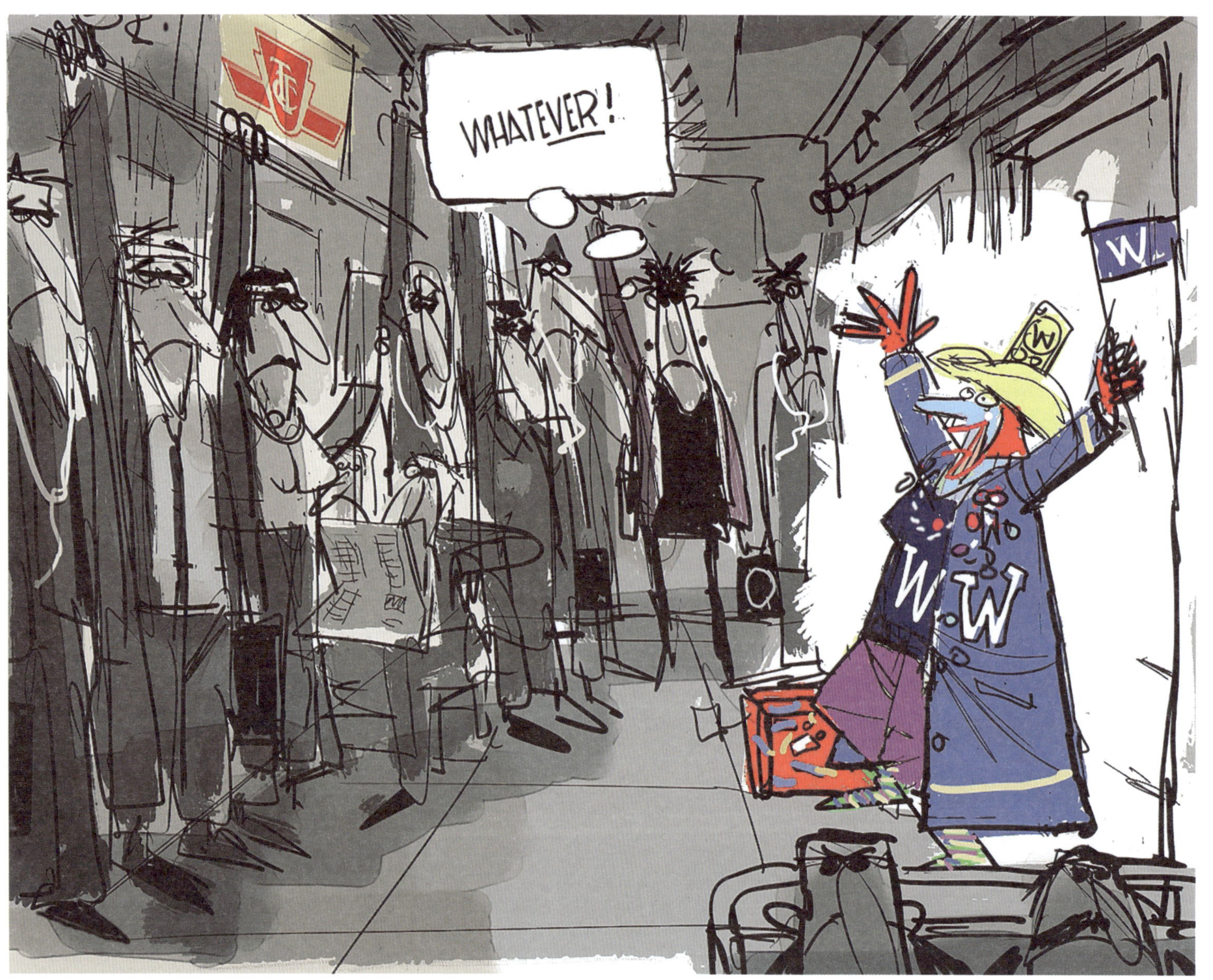
WHATEVER!
TTC
W
W
W W

During Grey Cup week in Toronto, 2007, I did a series of sketches of the week's events for the *Globe and Mail*.

In this drawing, a jubilant Winnipeg Blue Bombers fan steps on to a rush hour subway car and experiences an embrace of the warmth and hospitality for which the city is so famous.

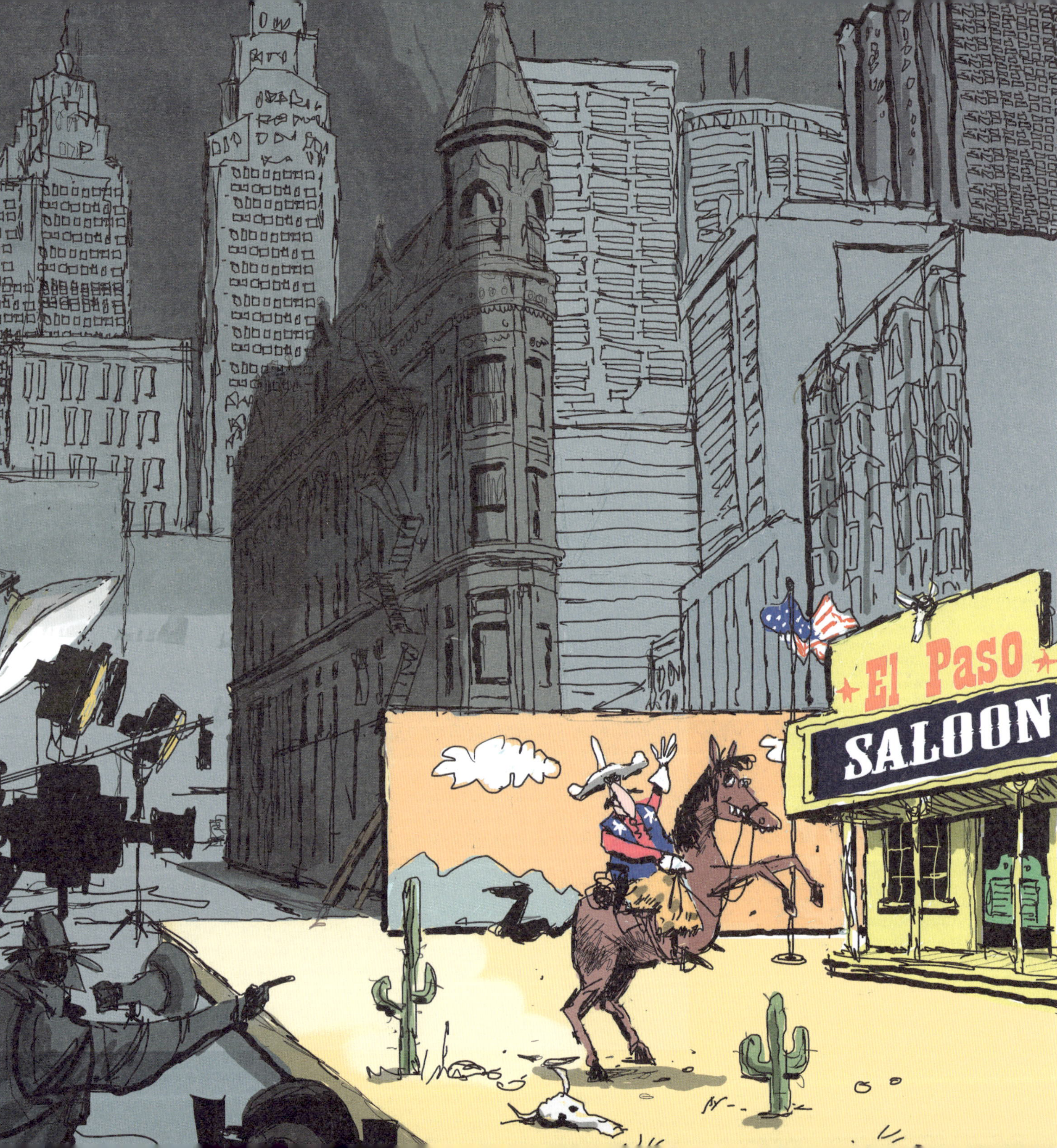
El Paso
SALOON

Because of Canada's frequently lower dollar and the city's generic appearance, Toronto becomes a stand-in for American settings in innumerable movies and TV shows.

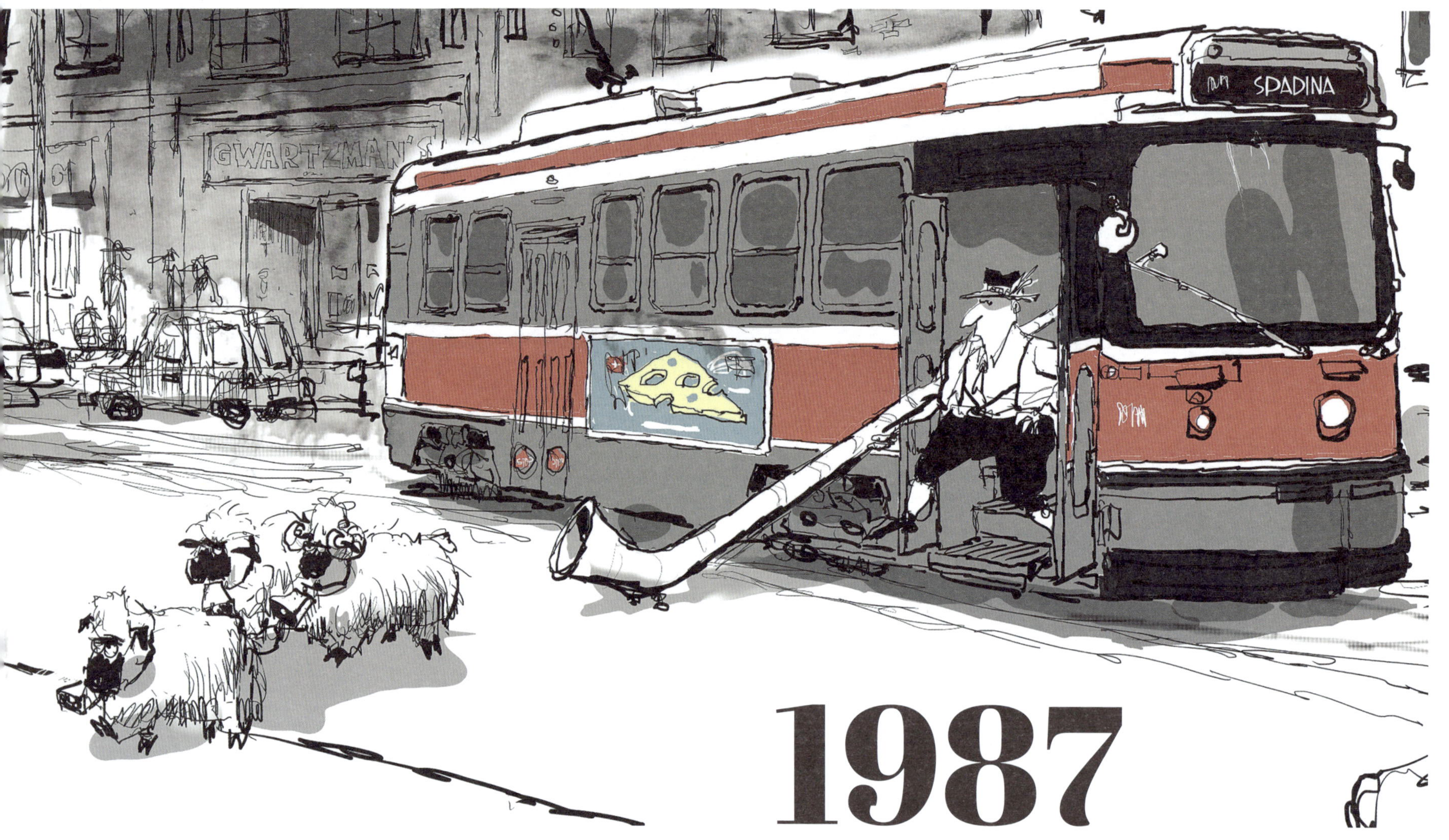

1987

"TORONTO IS A KIND OF NEW YORK RUN BY THE SWISS."

PETER USTINOV

1989

Skydome opens.

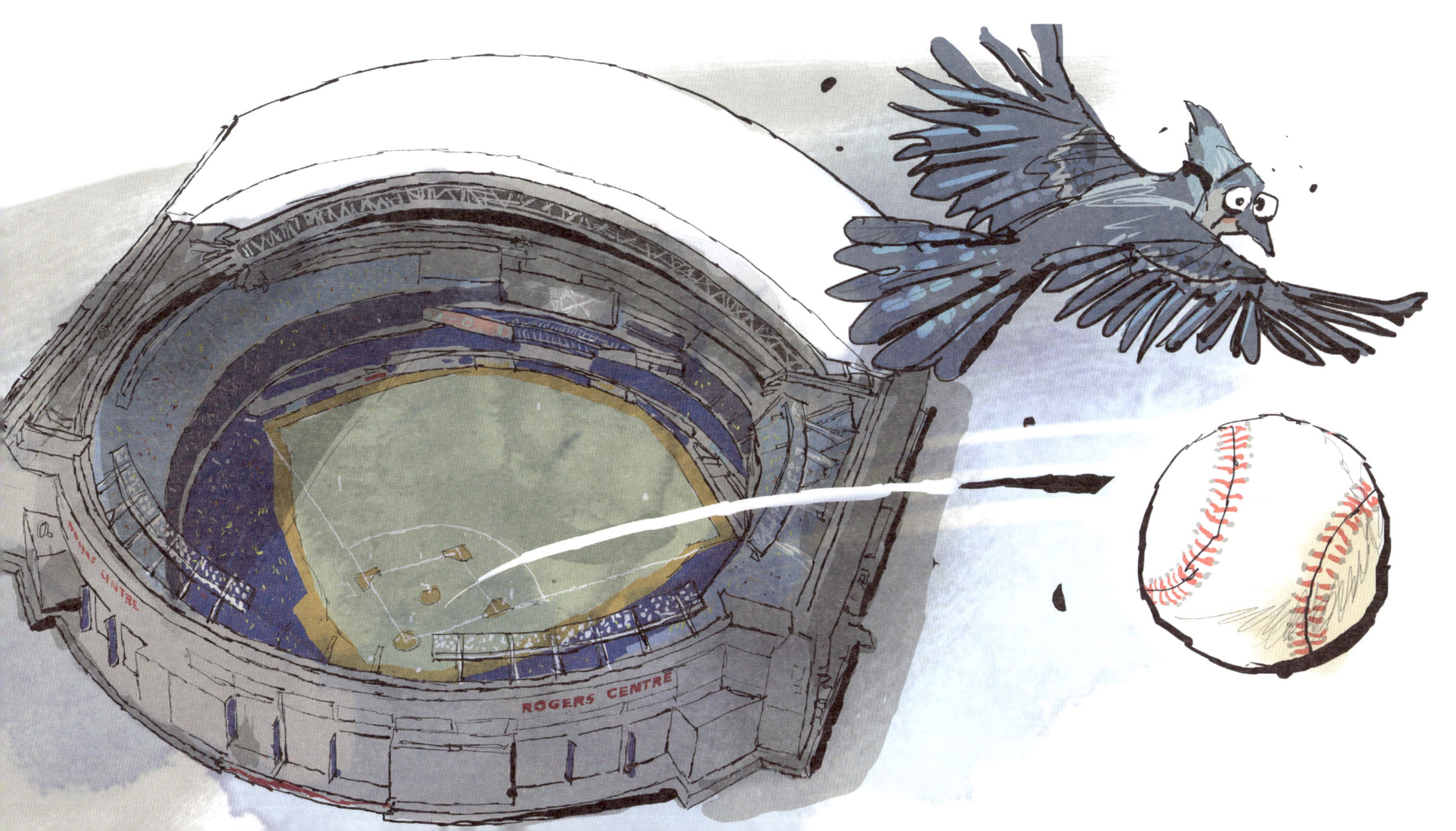

1992

Height and monumentality becomes the defining feature in many of the city's newly launched architectural projects. An example of this spirit of dramatic scale is the six-storey pedestrian walkway, "The Allen Lambert Galleria" connecting Bay Street to Sam Pollock Square in the heart of Toronto's commercial district.

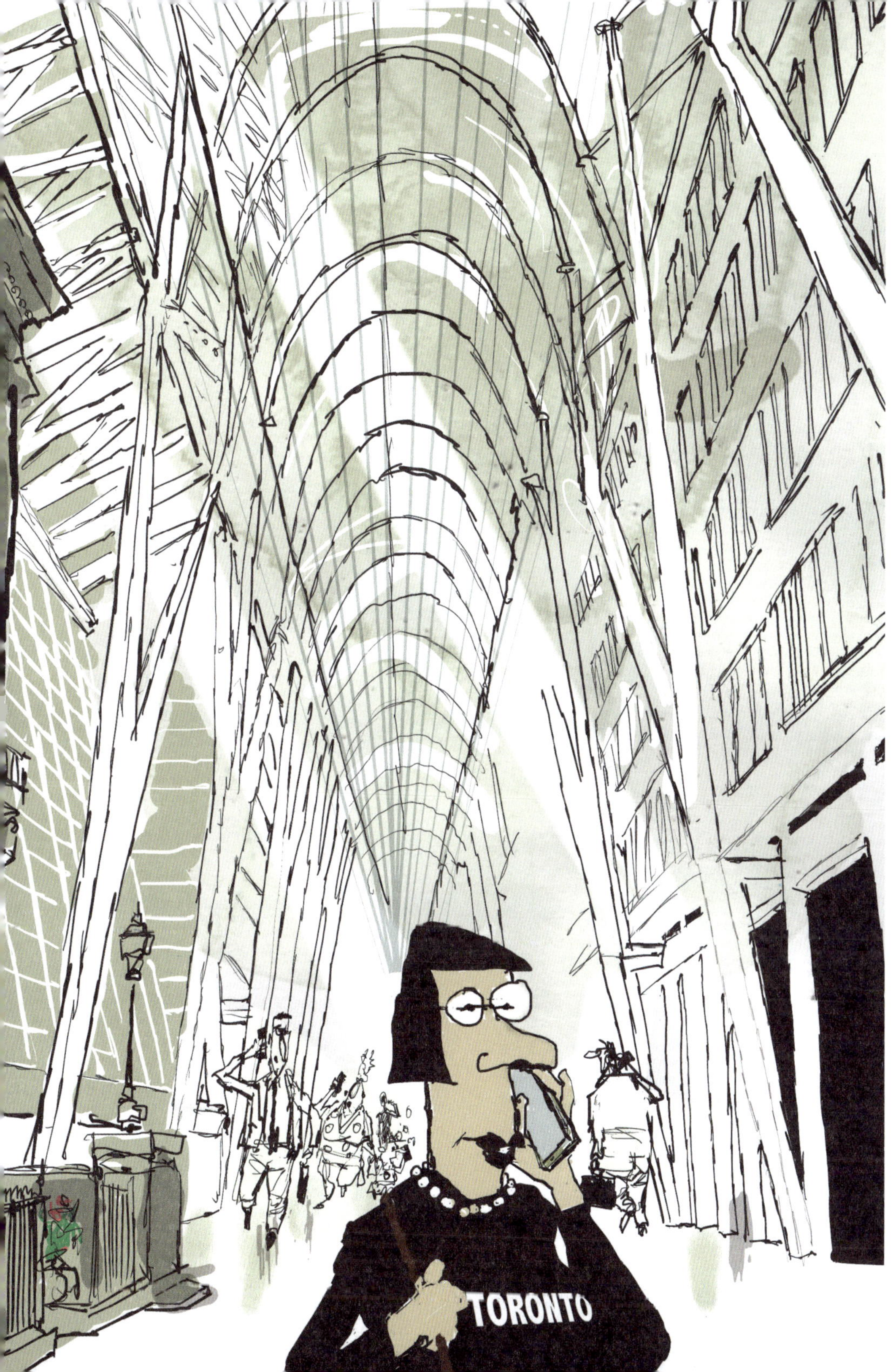
TORONTO

2000

THE CONSTRUCTION BOOM

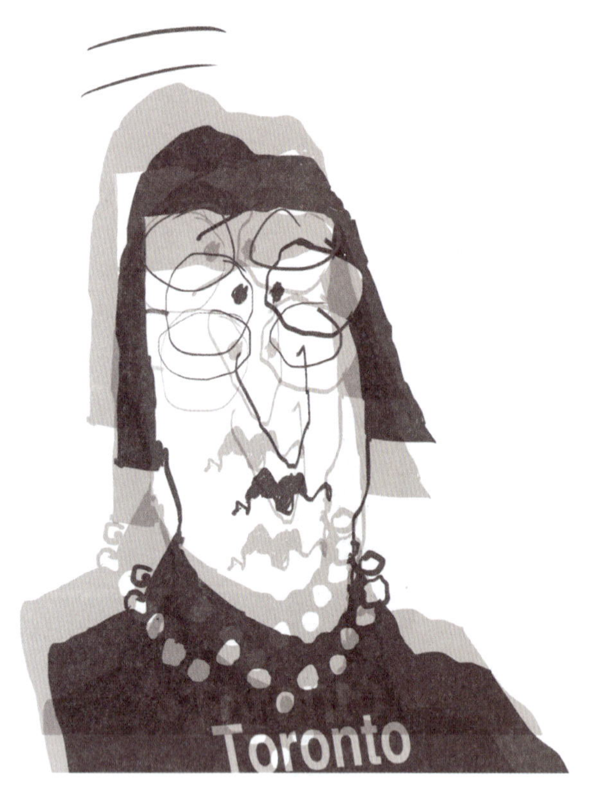

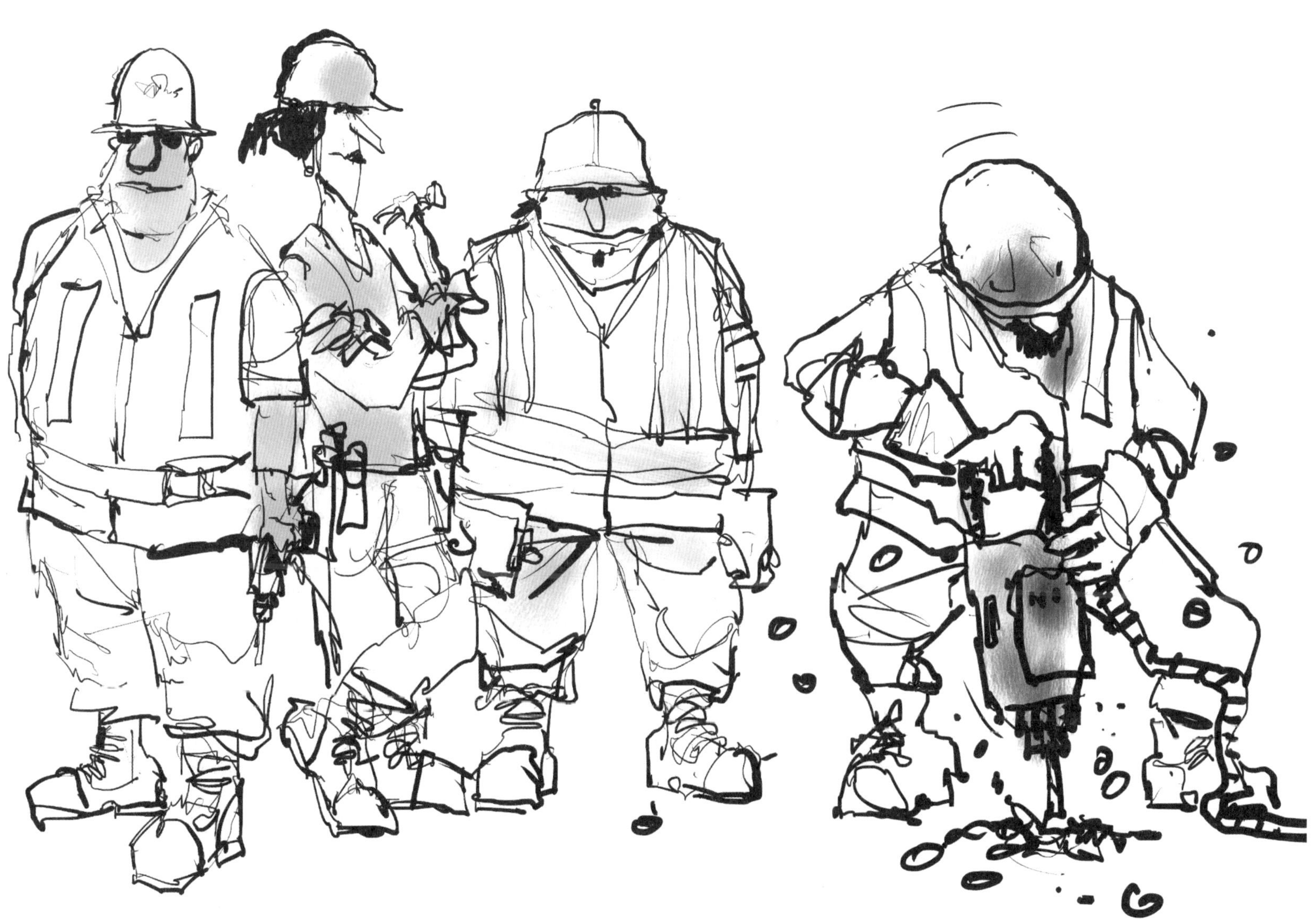

Sunset over
Lake Ontario

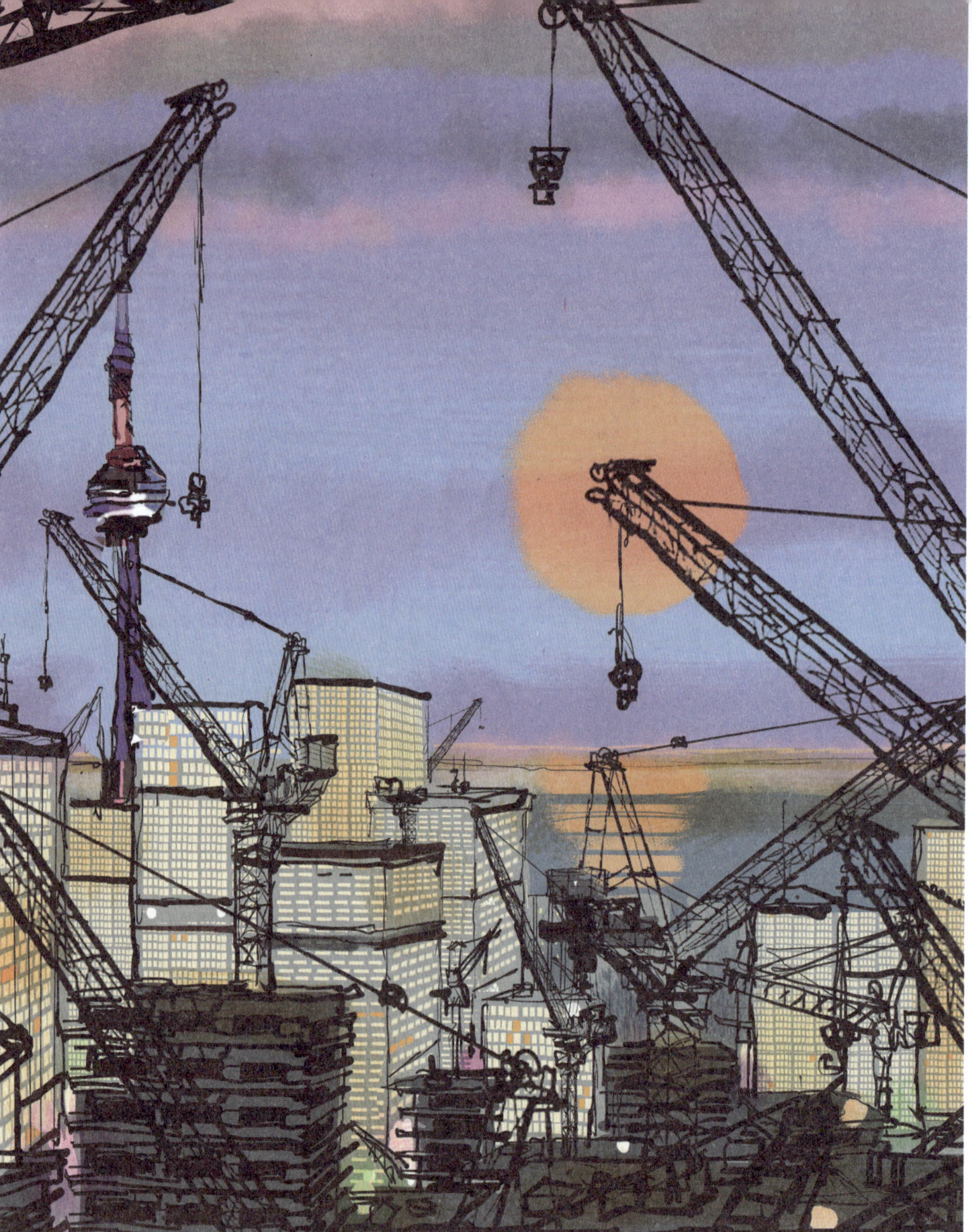

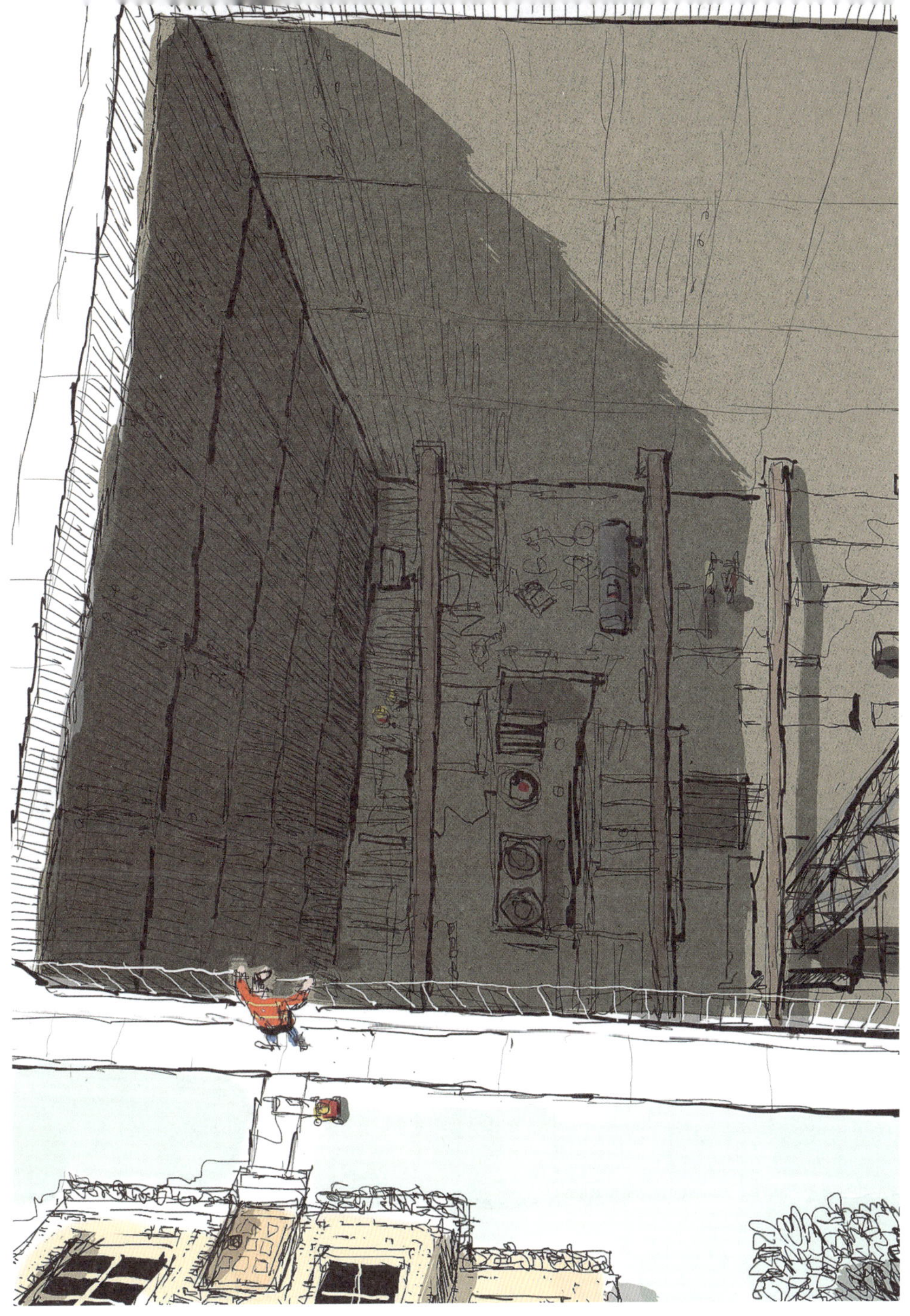

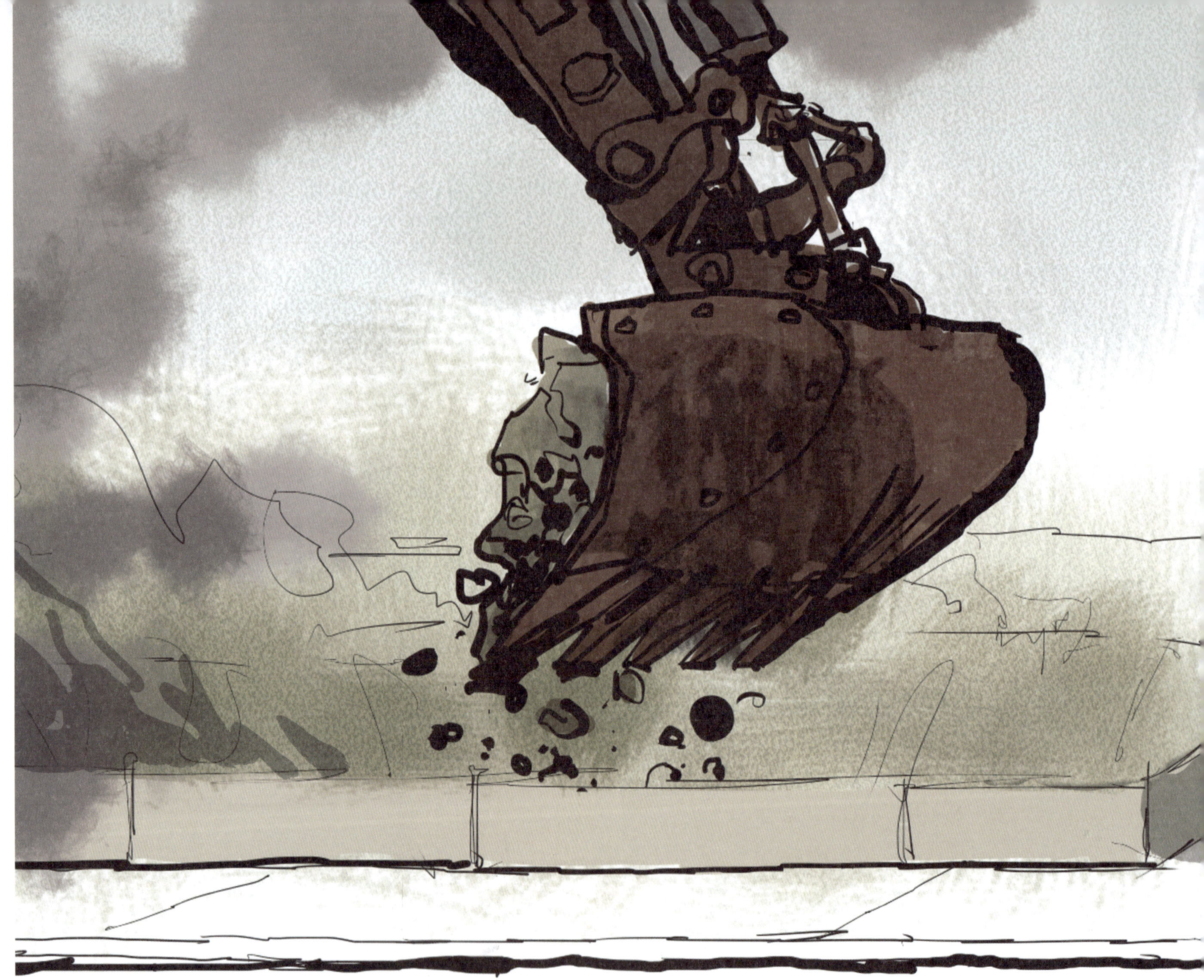

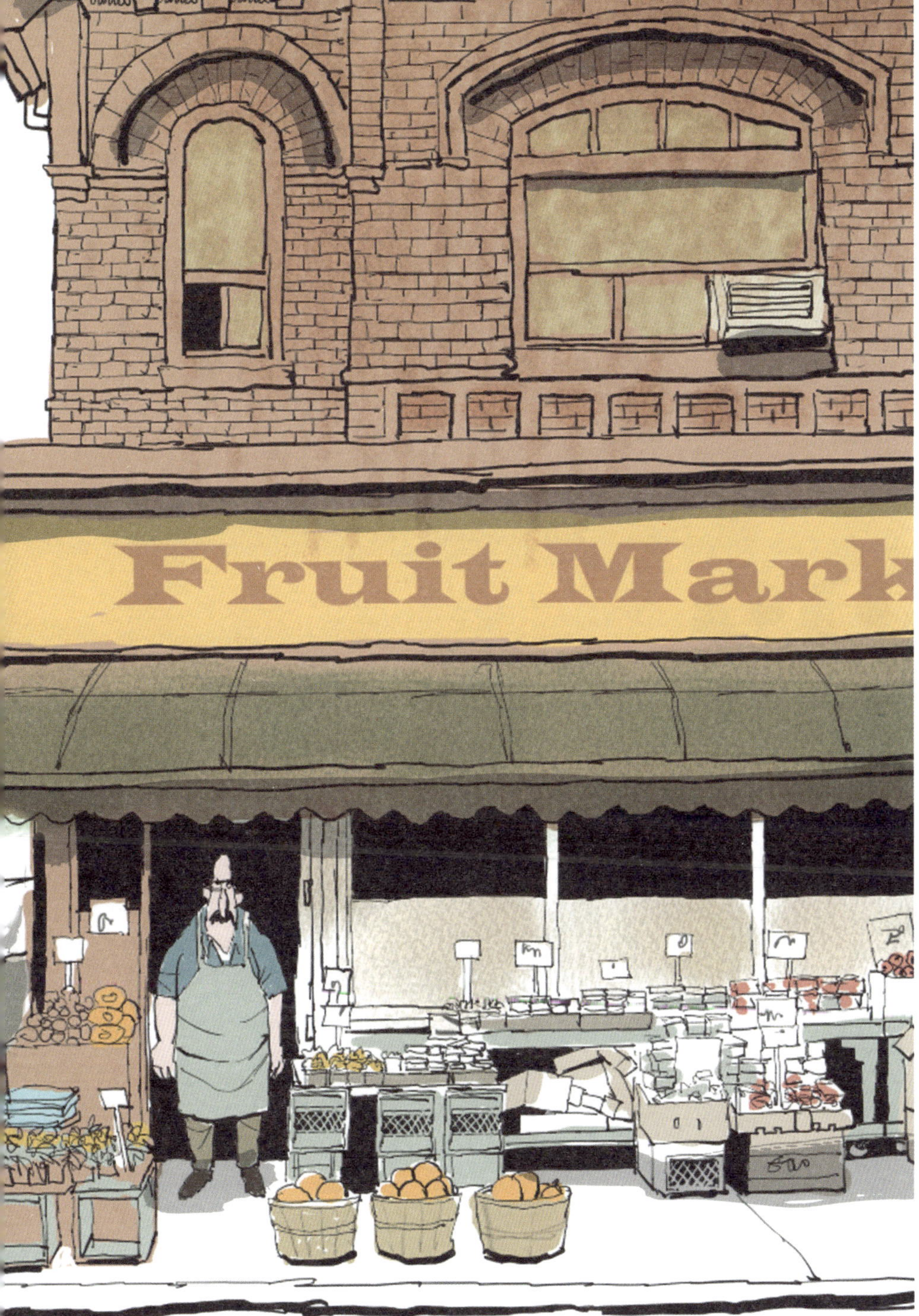

Here today . . .

. . . condo tomorrow

2022

Toronto gains attention for its growing international food scene.

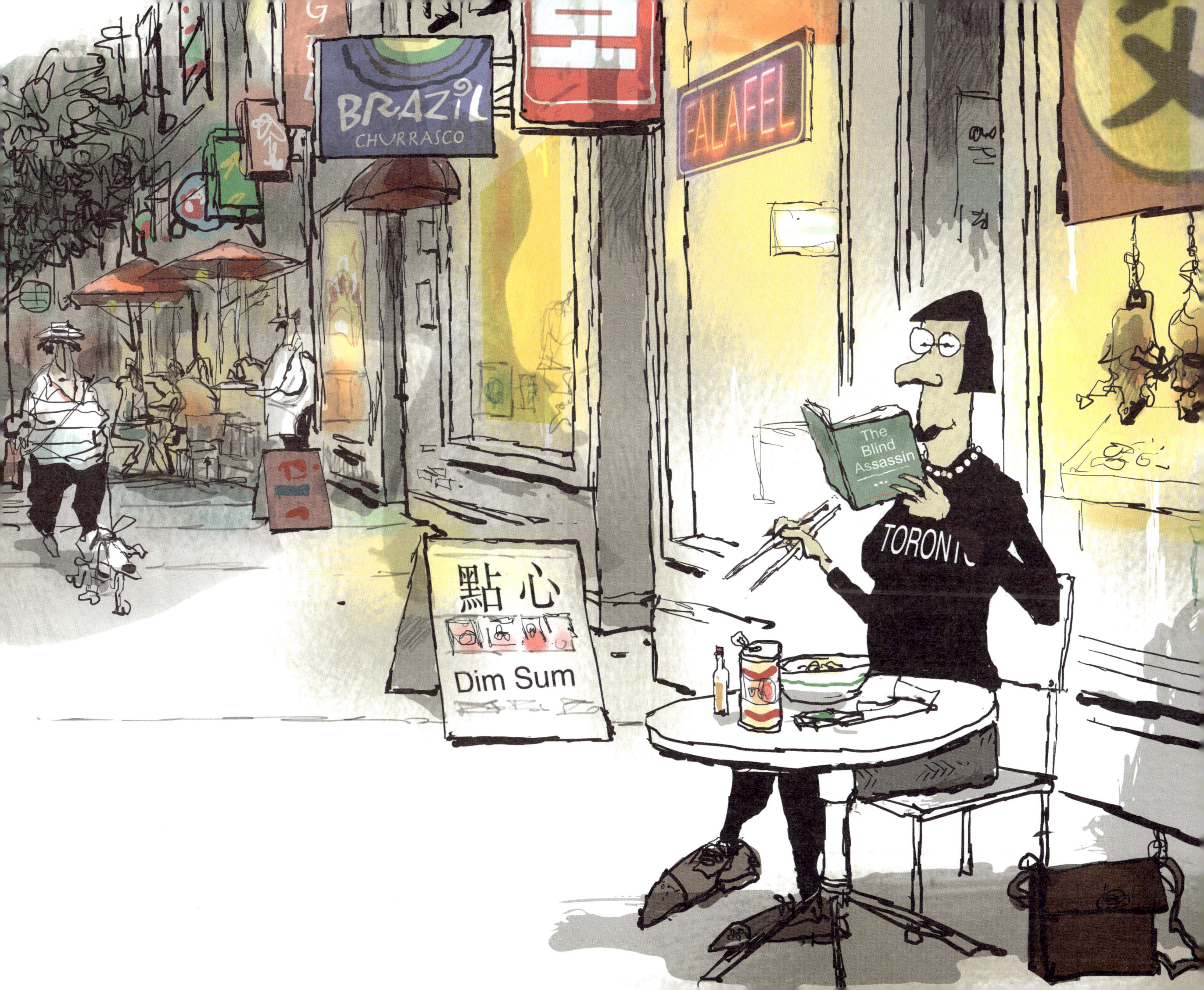
BRAZIL
CHURRASCO
FALAFEL
點心
Dim Sum
The Blind Assassin

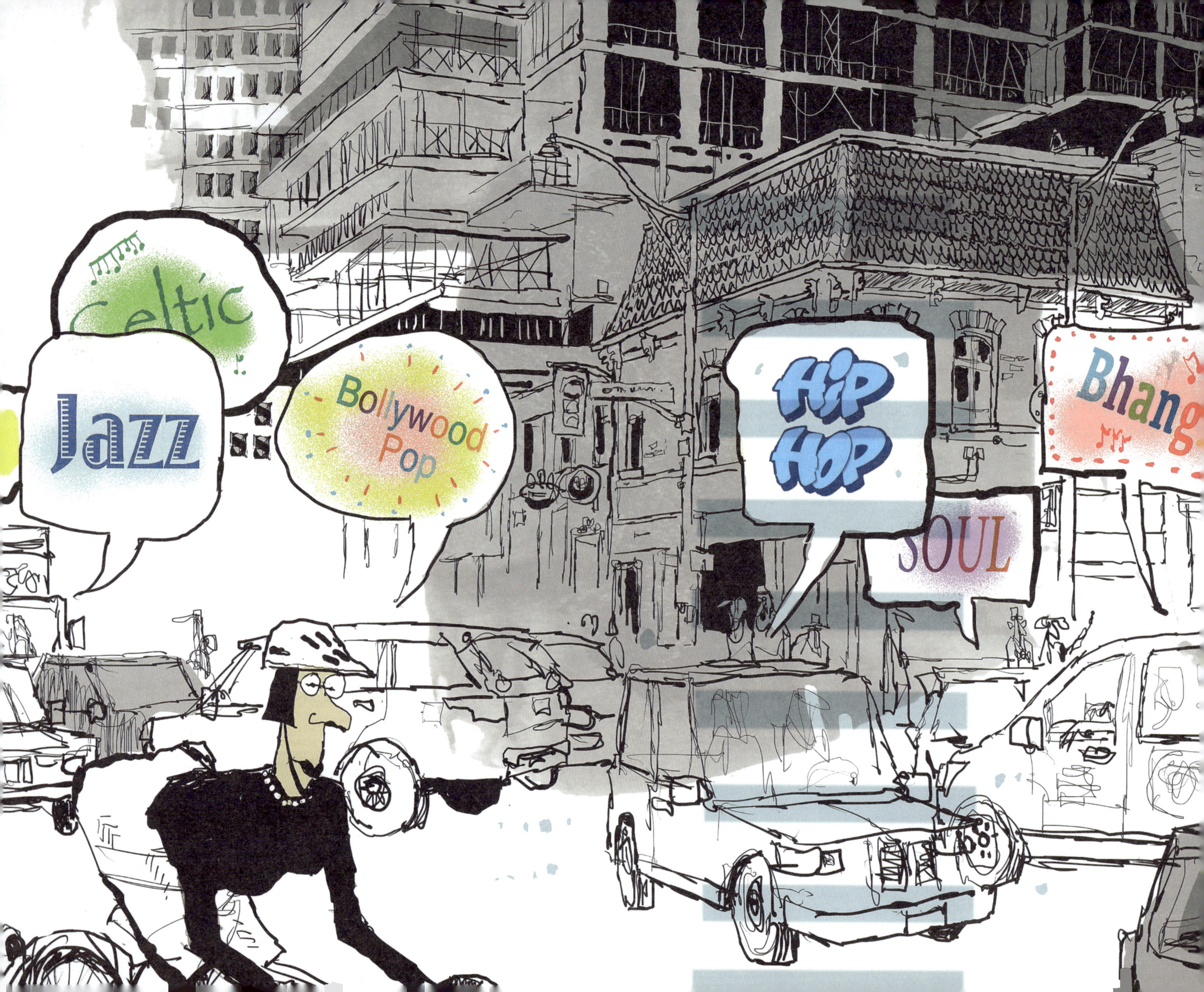
Celtic
Jazz
Bollywood Pop
Hip Hop
Soul
Bhang

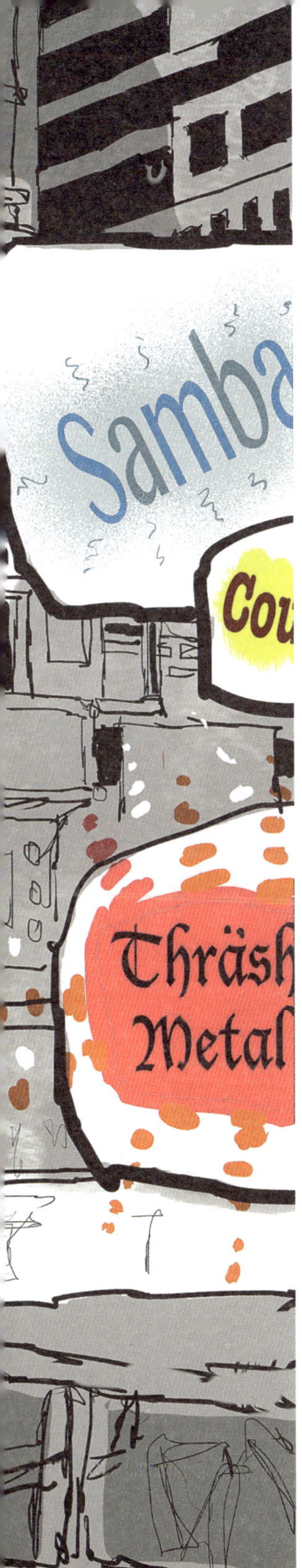

On a warm summer afternoon, when car windows are lowered and sunroofs are open, music from a multitude of nations fills the streets.

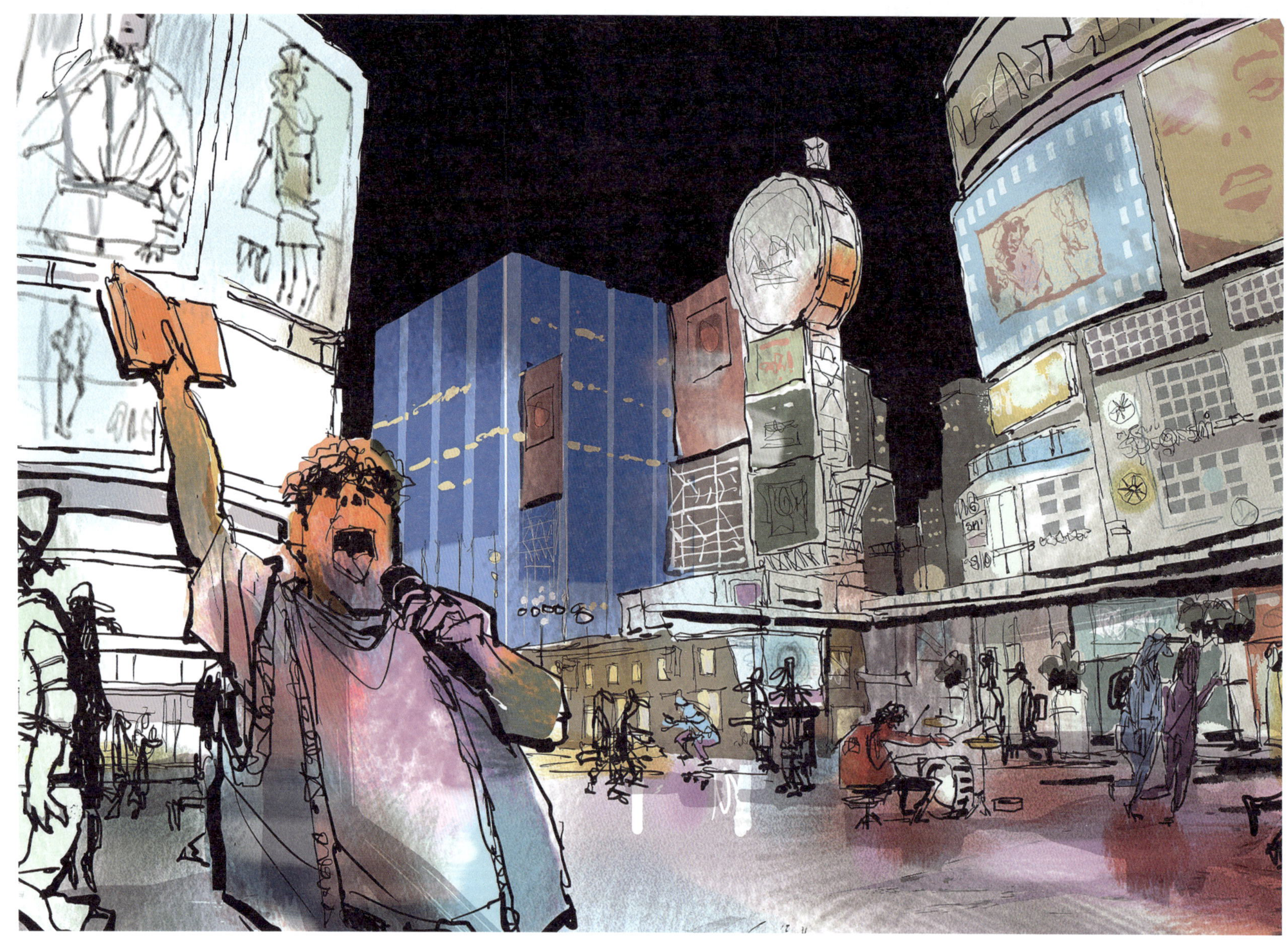

On a muggy August late night, the downtown streets resonate with a pulsing energy that is quintessentially urban.

There's a danger that Toronto risks losing the neighbourly ambience of its streetscapes. A feature that Jane Jacobs stressed was crucial for urban environments.

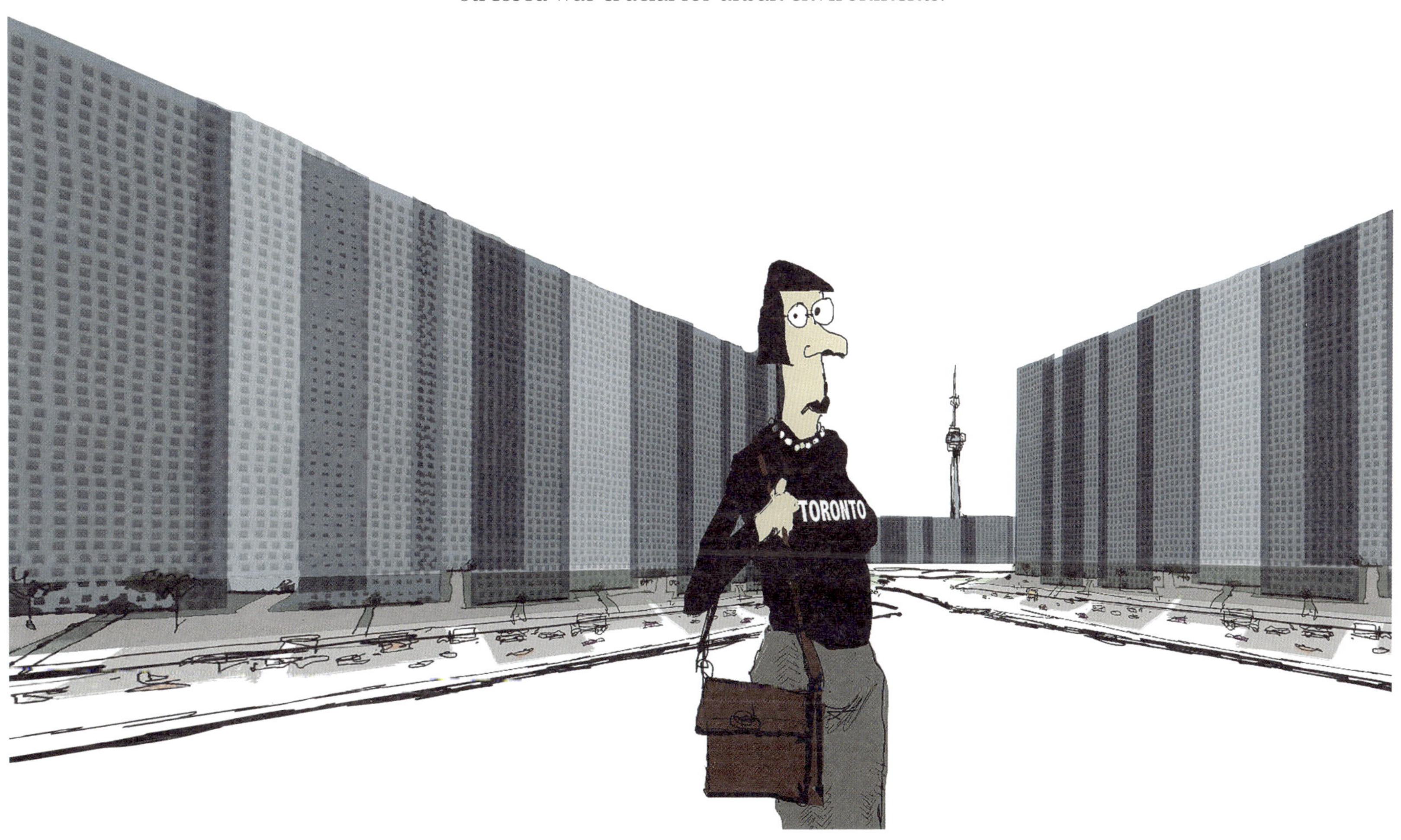

The city's relentless physical transformation has increasingly inspired a mood of self-reflection.

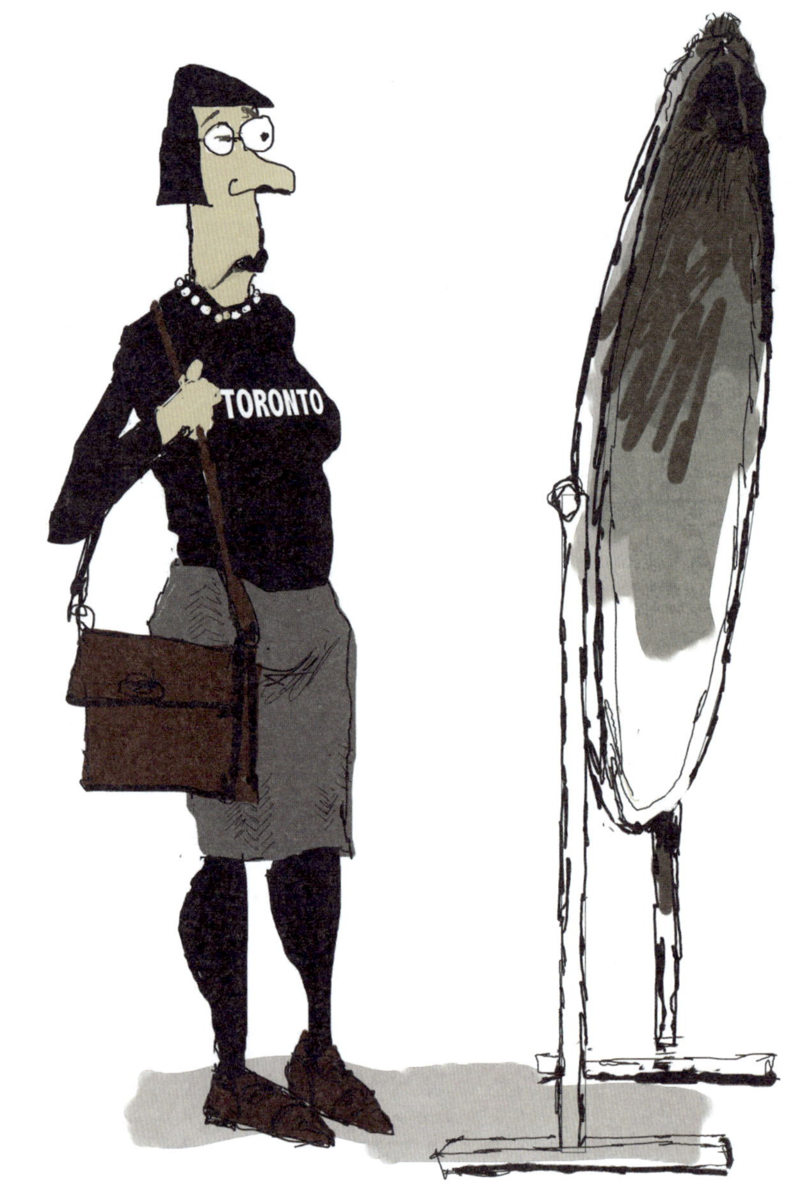

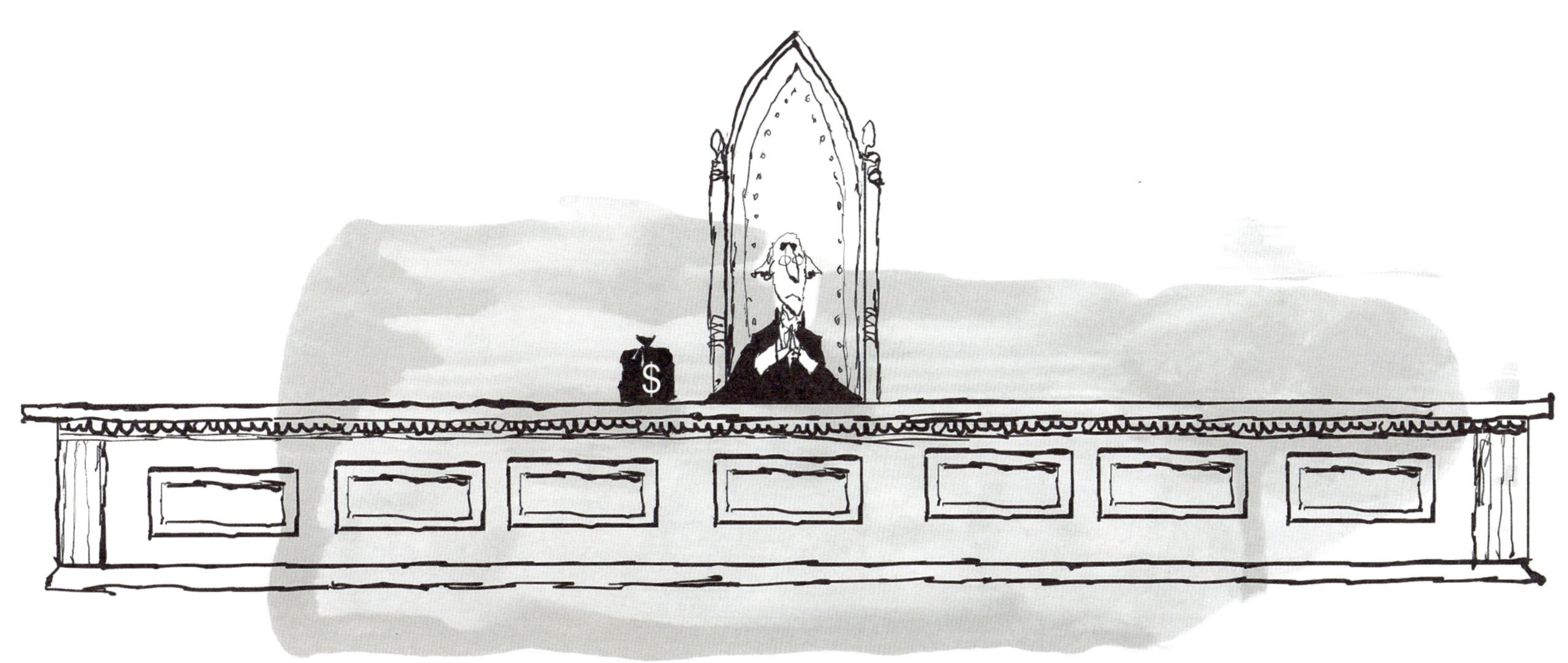

"I SEE CANADA AS A COUNTRY TORN BETWEEN A VERY NORTHERN, RATHER EXTRAORDINARY, MYSTICAL SPIRIT WHICH IT FEARS AND ITS DESIRE TO PRESENT ITSELF TO THE WORLD AS A SCOTCH BANKER."

ROBERTSON DAVIES

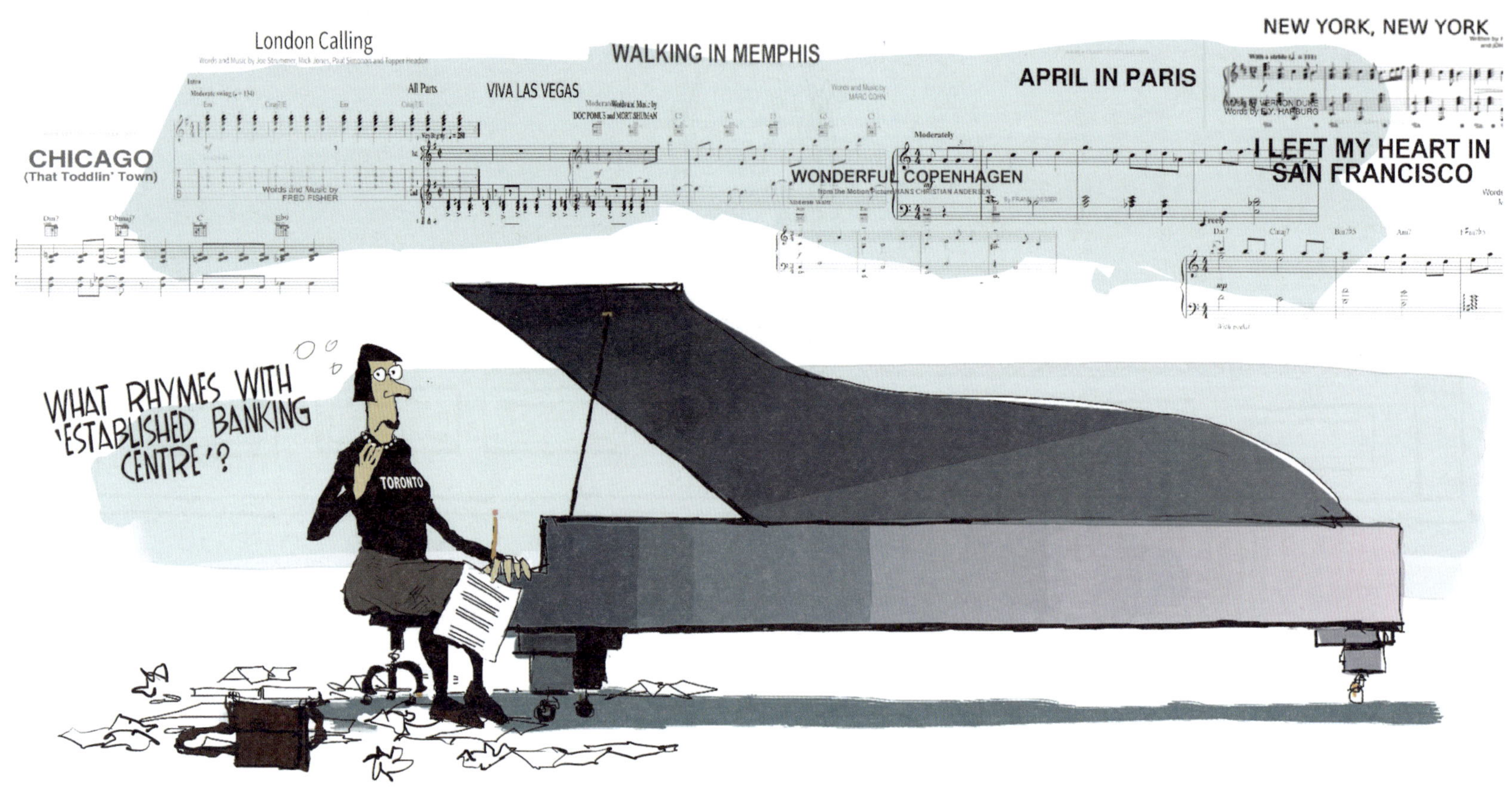

Perhaps one day the city's evolving character will inspire an anthem to its uniqueness?

IN THE END, THE ISSUE IS NOT WHETHER TORONTO HAS A CULTURE WORTH HAVING, BUT WHETHER TORONTO IS GOING TO BE AN URBAN COMMUNITY WORTH LIVING IN

THE RICH WANT MUCH SHOW-BIZZY URBAN GLAMOR – PRICEY OPERA HOUSES, FANTASTIC CONDOS, GLITZY ONE-SHOT FESTIVALS (SUCH AS THE TORONTO INTERNATIONAL FESTIVAL), COMPANIES FOR THE PERFORMANCE OF DEAD ART, SUCH AS CLASSICAL BALLET – BUT THEY SHOW LITTLE INCLINATION TO PUT OUT THE MONEY, TIME AND WORK NECESSARY TO NUTURE TORONTO'S MOST ADVANCED ARTS AND PUT THE CITY ON A STEADY COURSE OUT OF ITS SELF-SATISFIED CULTURAL MEDIOCRITY.

WELCOME TO TORONTO, AS THE RICH WANT IT TO BE: CLEVELAND IN RHINESTONE DRAG.

JOHN BENTLEY MAYS 1986

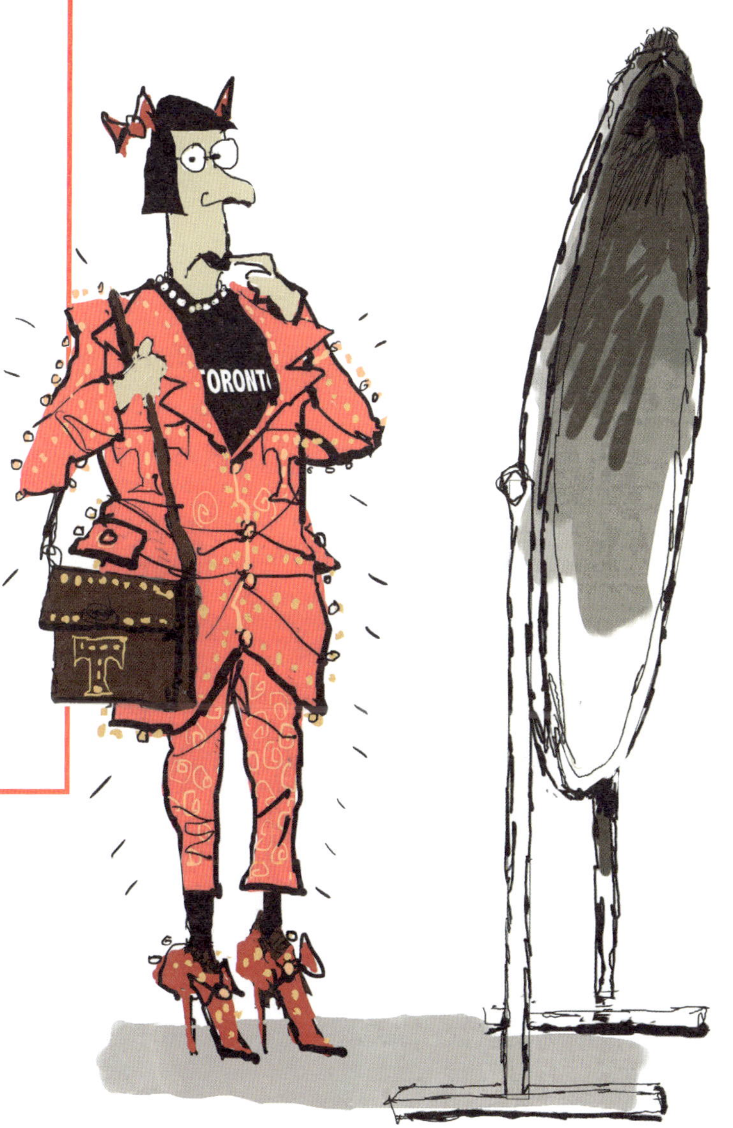

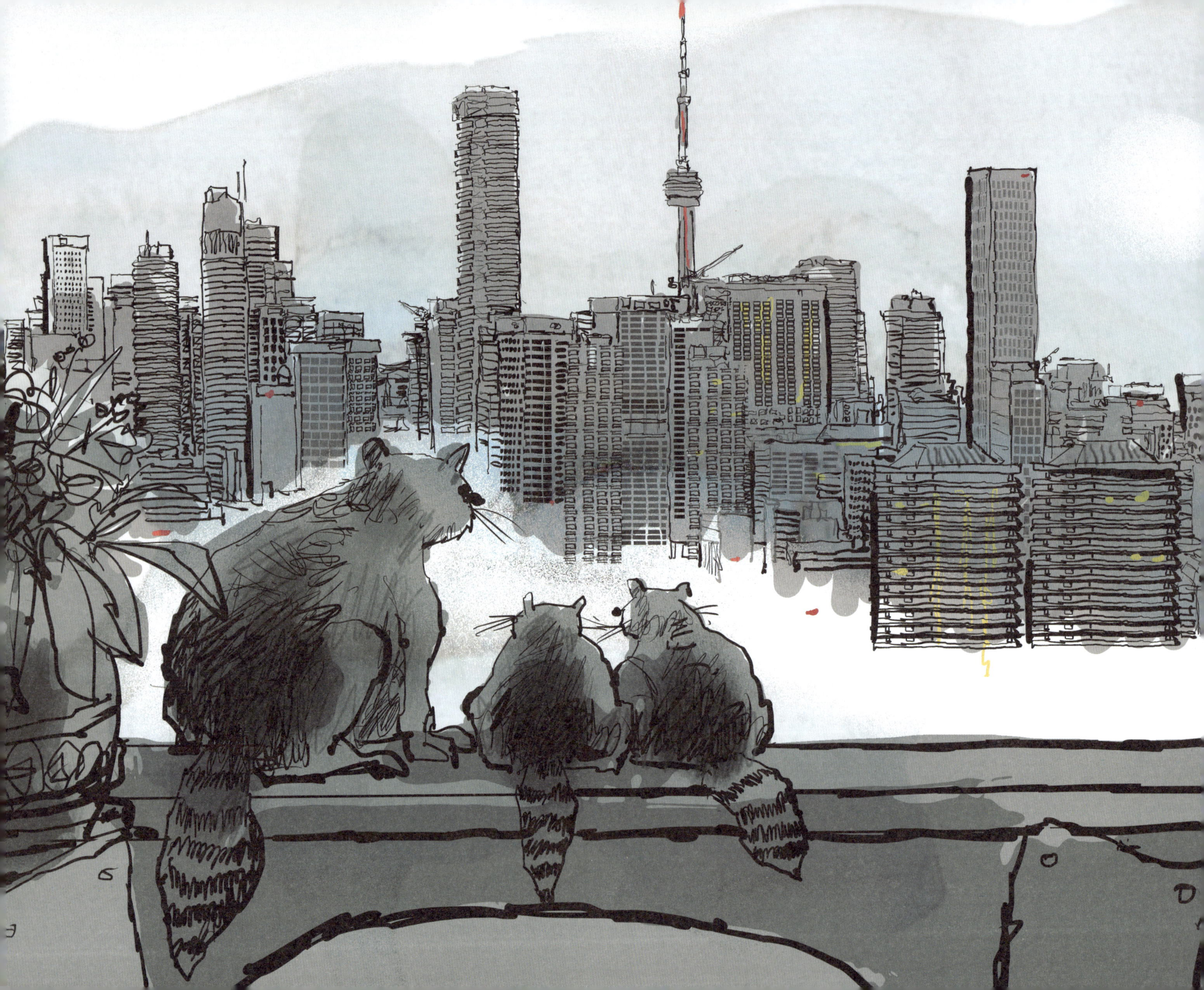

WHITHER TORONTO?

Cities come and go. Some, like Rome, survive for millennia. Others come to untimely ends, occasionally under mysterious circumstances. Most cities undergo radical transformations for better and for worse.

Immediately after World War II, Jan Morris felt an overwhelming affection for London. It was scarred by the blitz and pockmarked with ruins, yet for her it symbolized nobility, strength and defiance. As the century moved on she watched London evolve into what she felt was an "invigorating dystopia."

So it goes.

This is a century of unprecedented migrations, comings and goings. Toronto has demonstrated an ability to absorb successive waves of new arrivals in a way that may have surprised a citizen of the mid-nineteenth century. This ability to welcome the new and to weave it into the existing fabric of the city may turn out to be one of Toronto's most positive virtues.

Here's hoping.

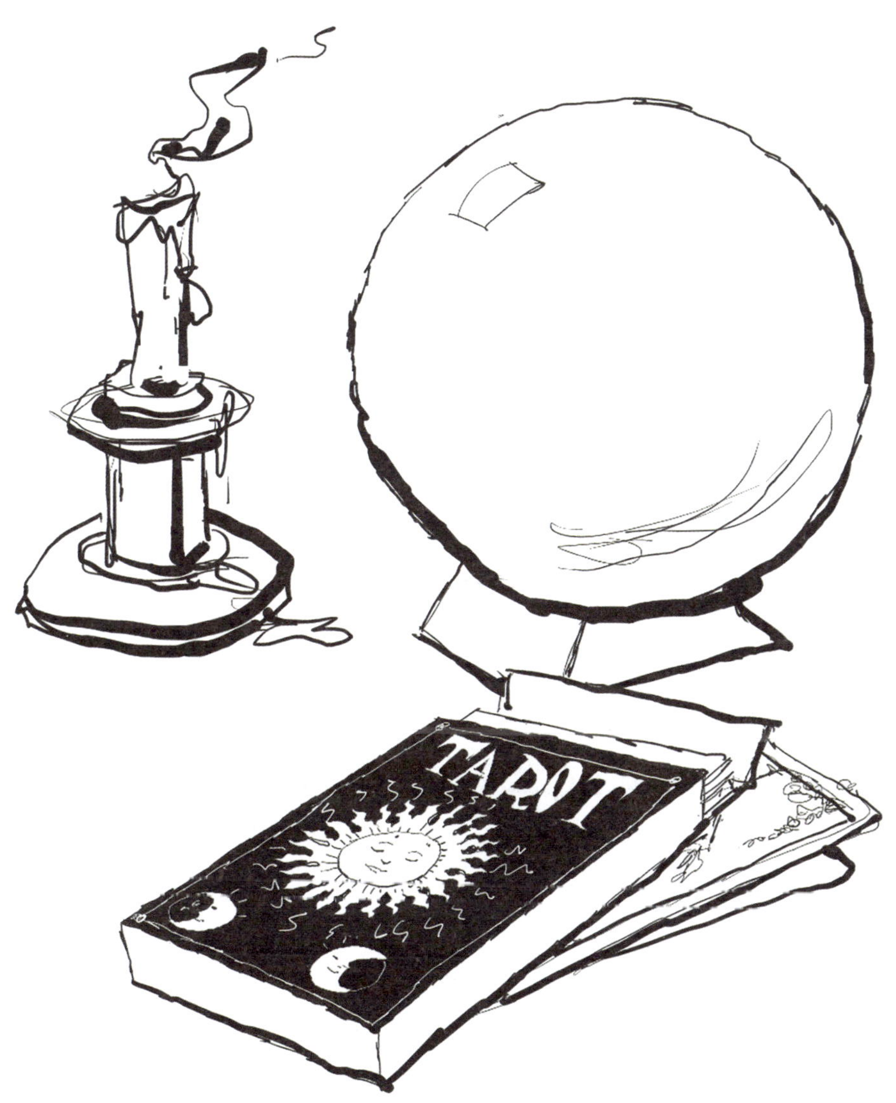

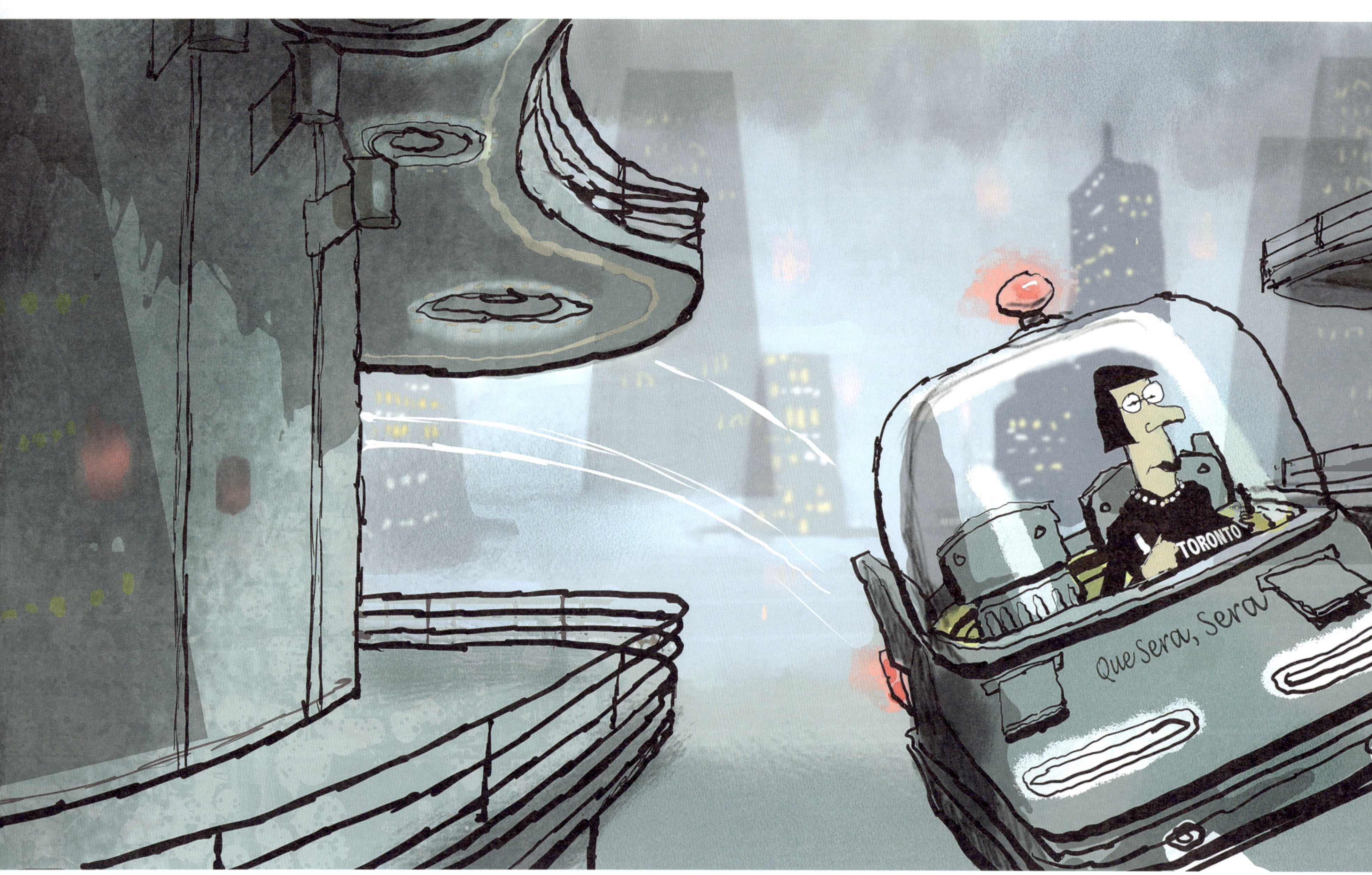
TORONTO
Que Sera, Sera

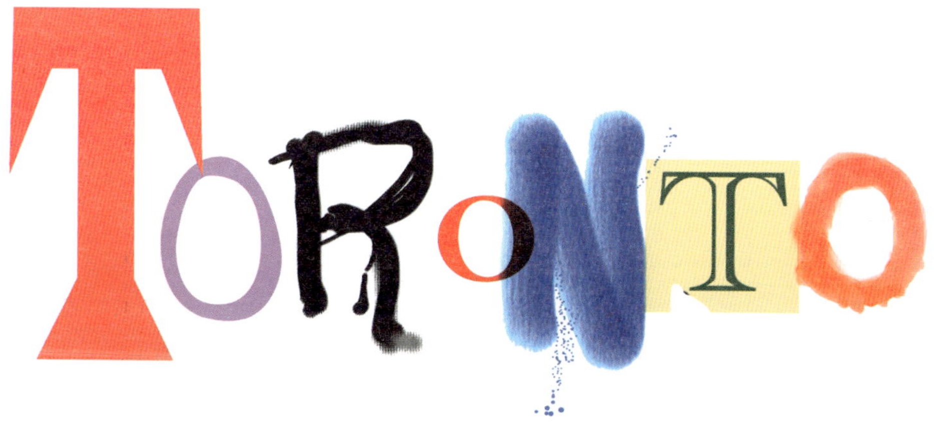
TORONTO